DRAWING BLOOD

CARTOONS FOR AMNESTY INTERNATIONAL

GRUB STREET · LONDON

Published by Grub Street, The Basement, 10 Chivalry Road, London SW11 1HT.

British Library Cataloguing in Publication Data
Drawing Blood: Cartoon Collection
Published in Association with Amnesty International
741.59

ISBN 1-898697-10-8

Printed and bound in Great Britain by Biddles Ltd., Guildford and King's Lynn.

The opinions expressed in this book are those of the individual cartoonists and not necessarily those of Amnesty International.

The publishers wish to thank Ralph Steadman for drawing the cover and all the following cartoonists for so generously agreeing to allow their work to be reproduced in this book:

Ros Asquith
David Austin
Jeremy Banx
Les Barton
Neil Bennett
Simon Bond
Kate Charlesworth
Clive Collins
Stan Eales
Barry Fantoni
Noel Ford
Martin Honeysett
Tony Husband
Chic Jacob
Larry
David Langdon
Annie Lawson
Chris Madden
Angela Martin
Nick Newman
Giles Pilbrow
John Power
Bryan Reading
Arthur Reid
David Shenton
Posy Simmonds
Jackie Smith
Carol Swain
Geoff Thompson
Robert Thompson
Paul Trotman
Mike Turner
Jim Unger
Patrick Wright

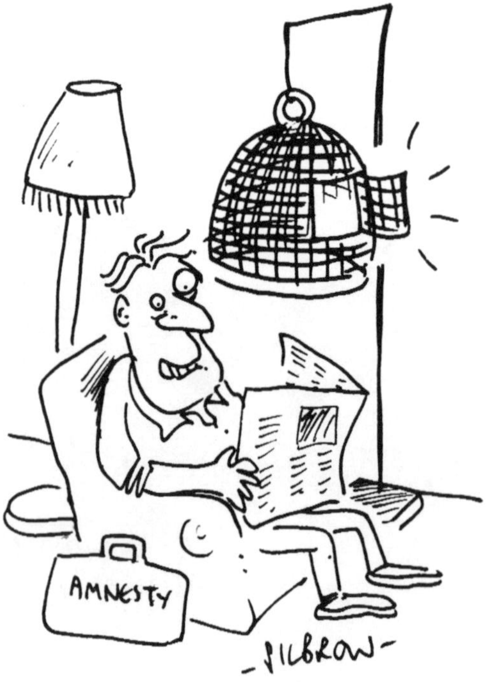
AMNESTY
PILBROW

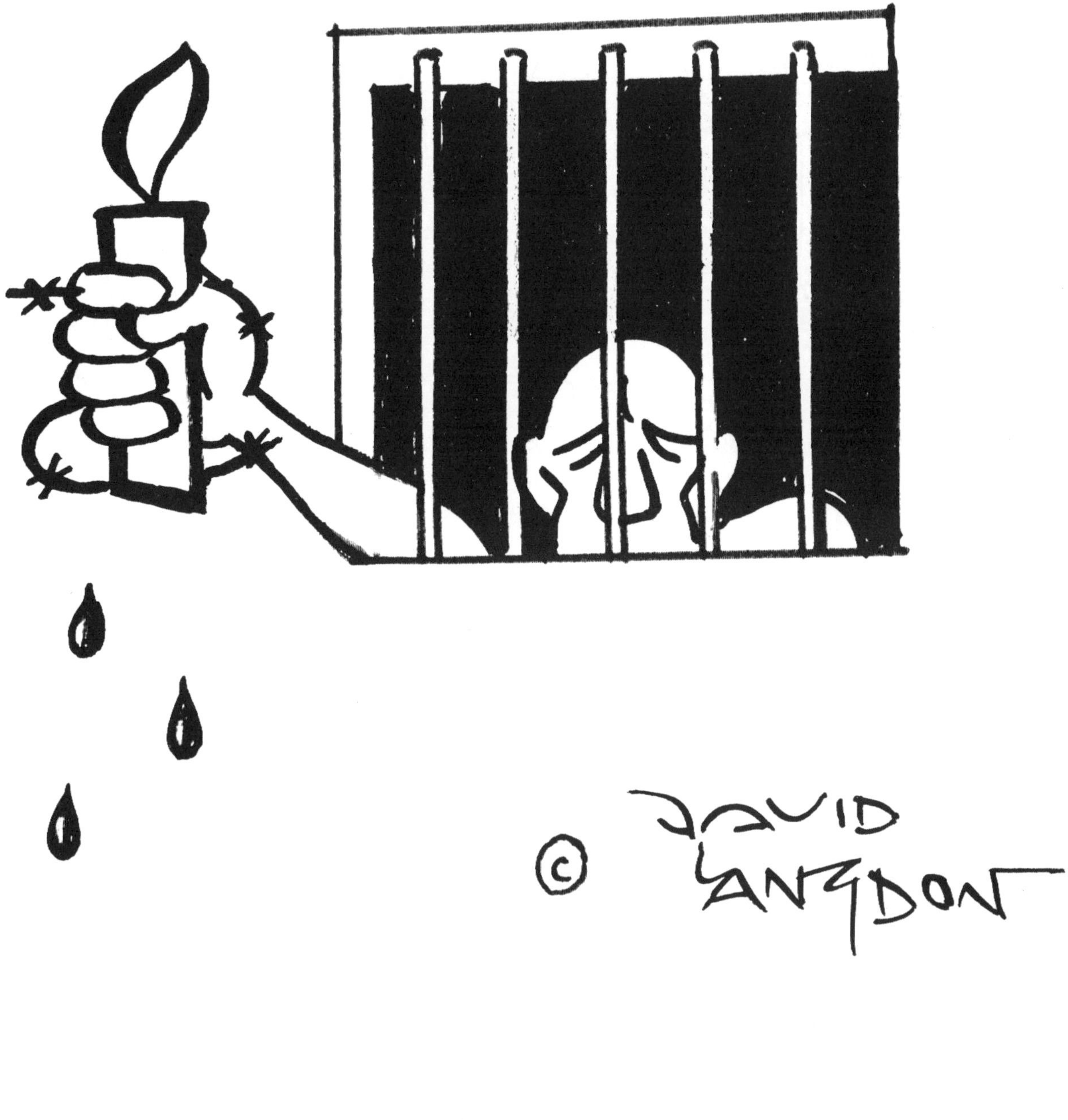
© DAVID LANGDON

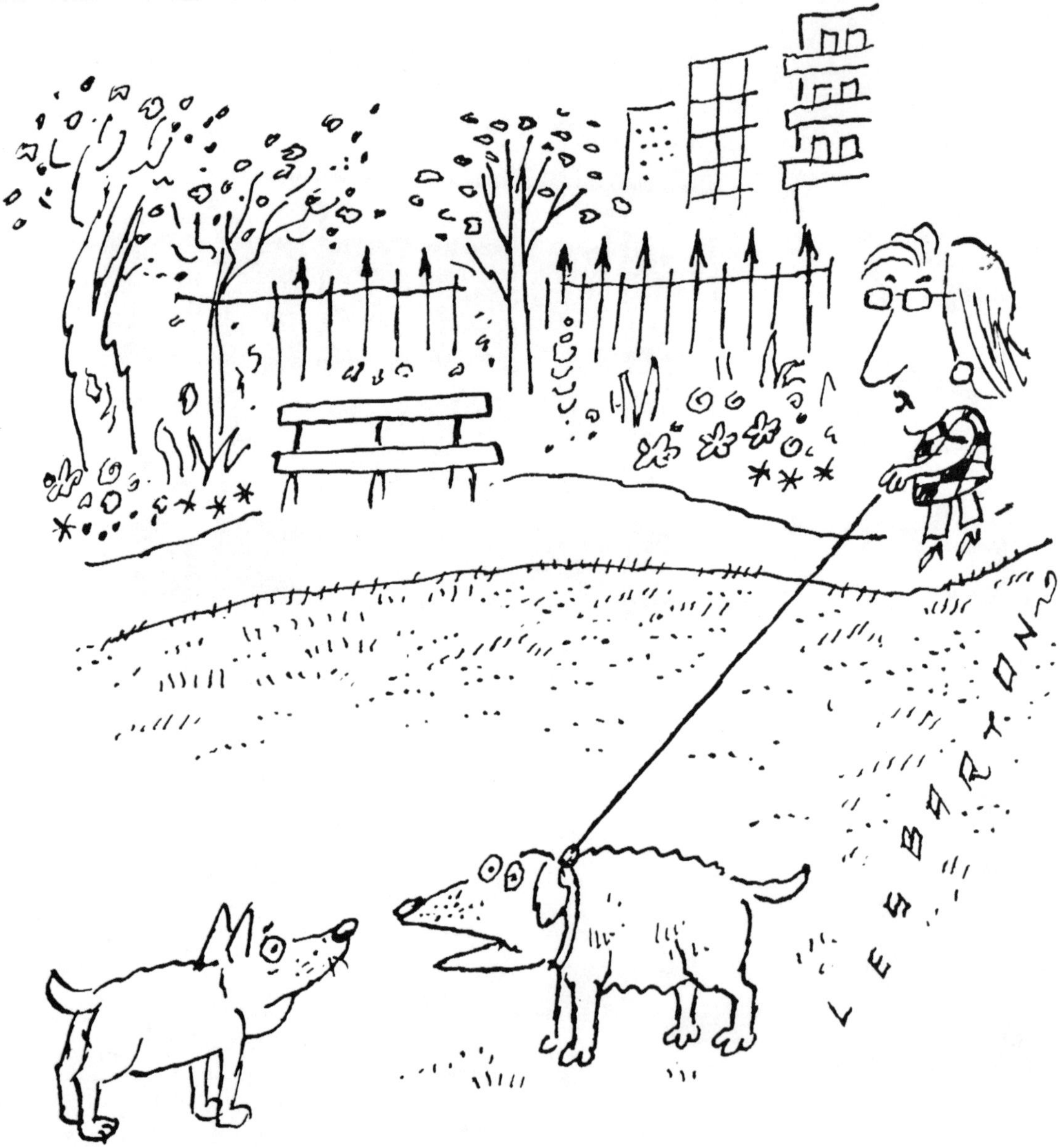
LES BARTON

'You can run but you can't hide!'

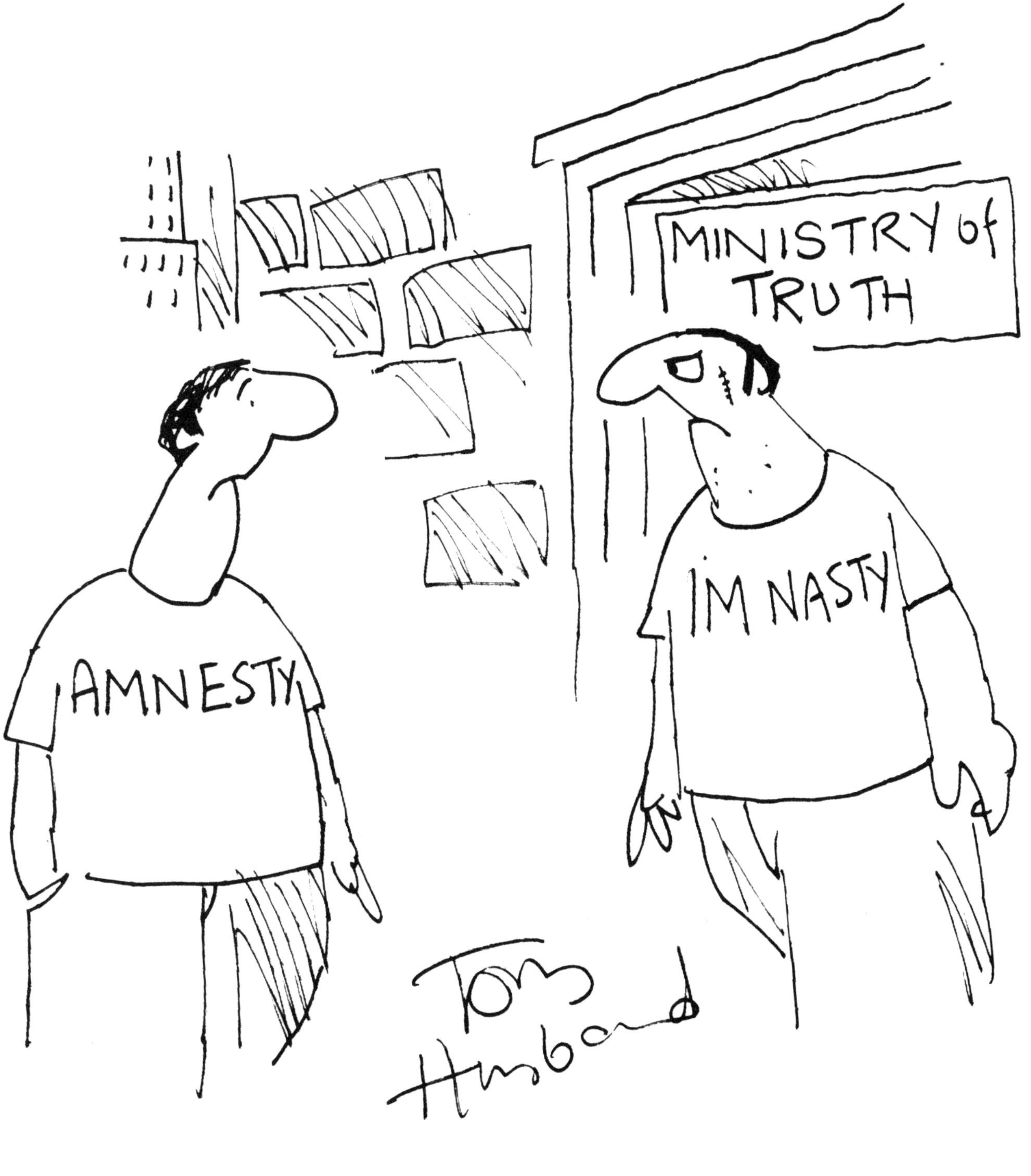
MINISTRY of TRUTH
AMNESTY
IM NASTY
Tom Husband

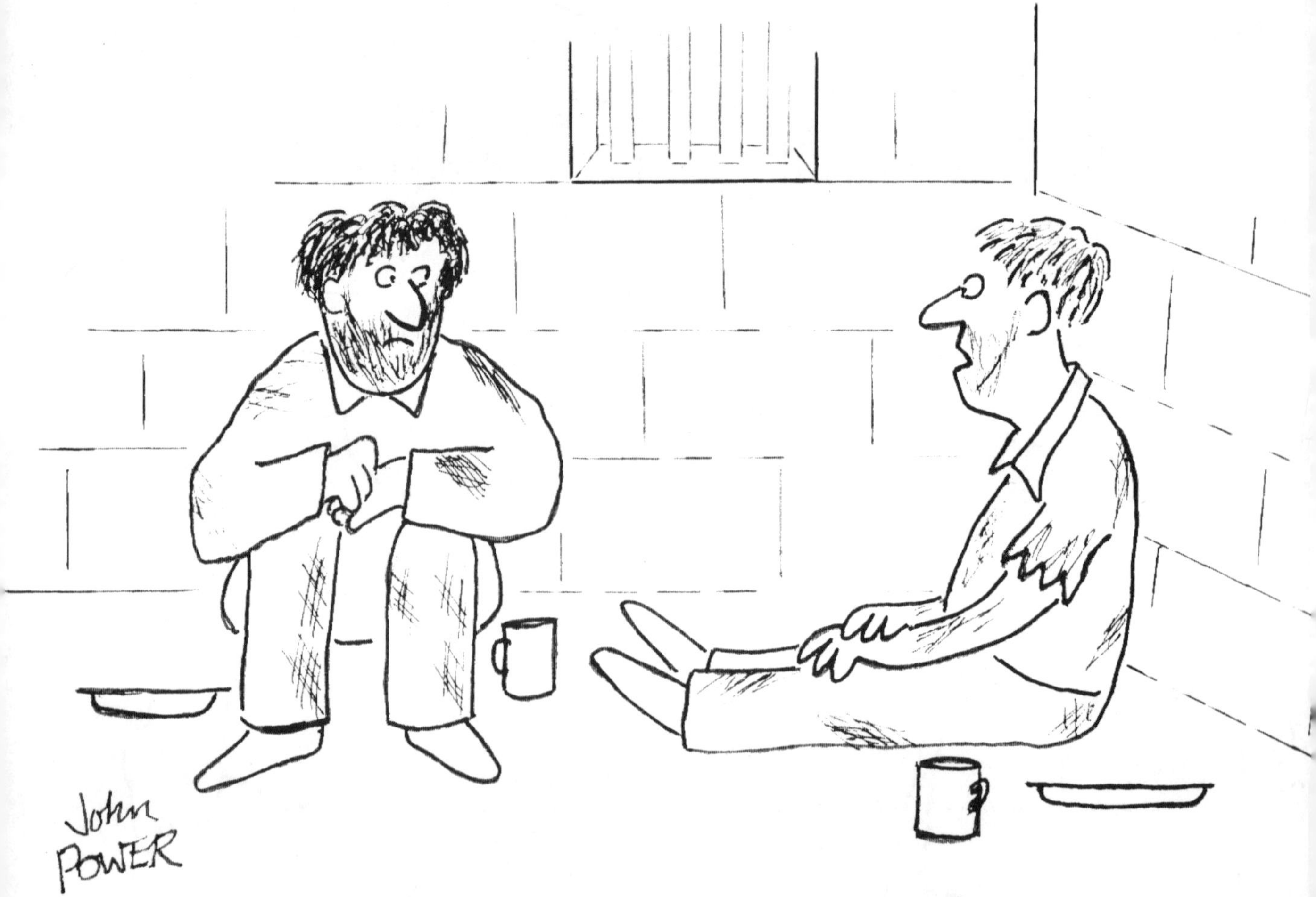
John POWER

'I held out against the beatings and electric shocks but then they forced me to watch ***Neighbours****'*

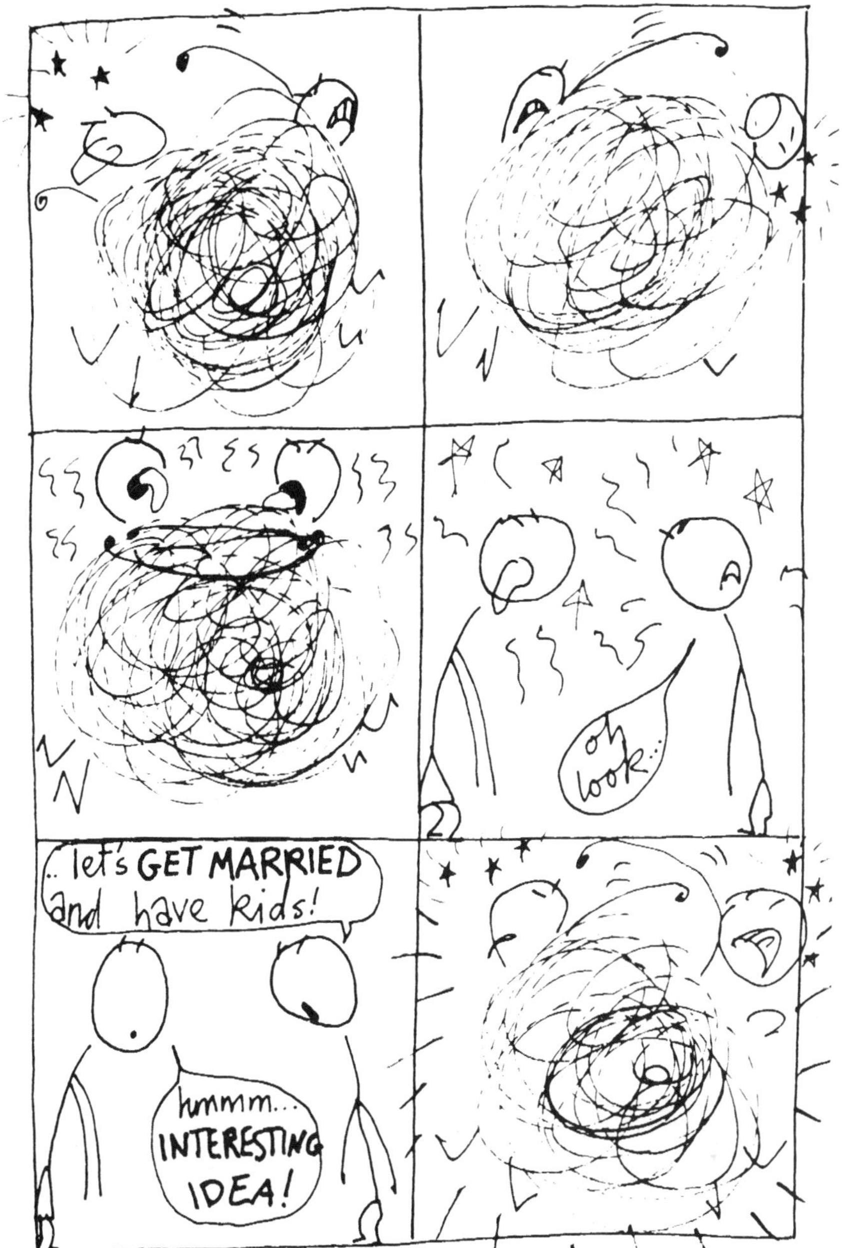

oh look...
.. let's GET MARRIED and have kids!
hmmm... INTERESTING IDEA!

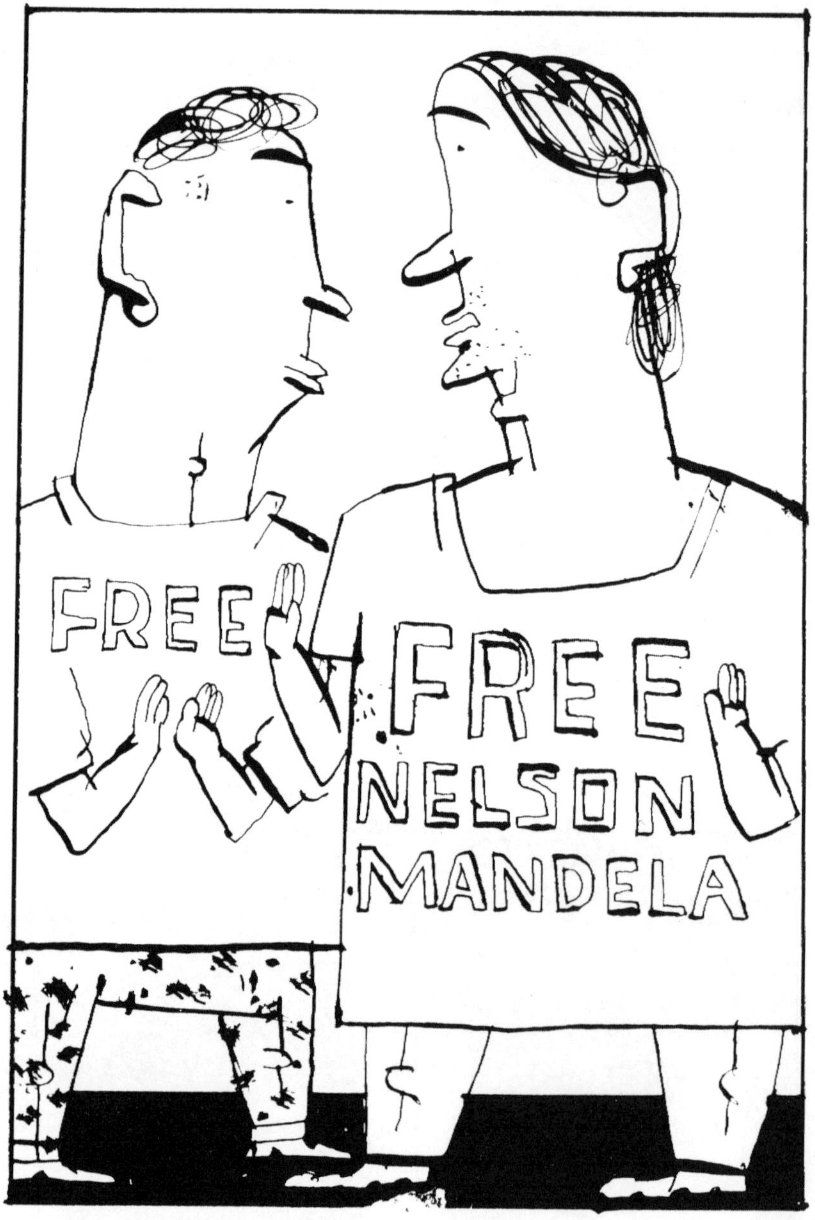
FREE
FREE
NELSON
MANDELA

'Er, what now?'

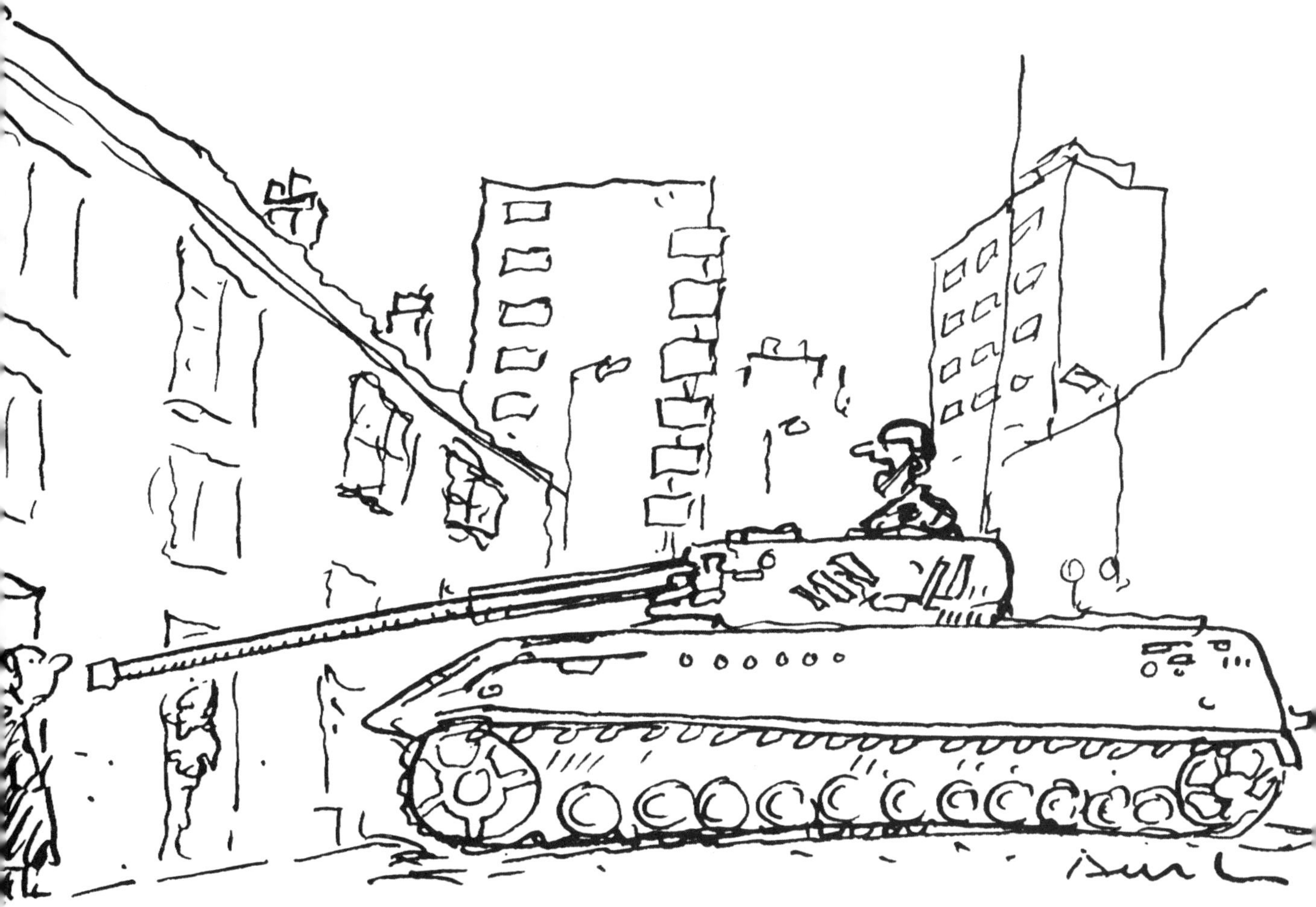

'Can we rely on your vote in the forthcoming election?'

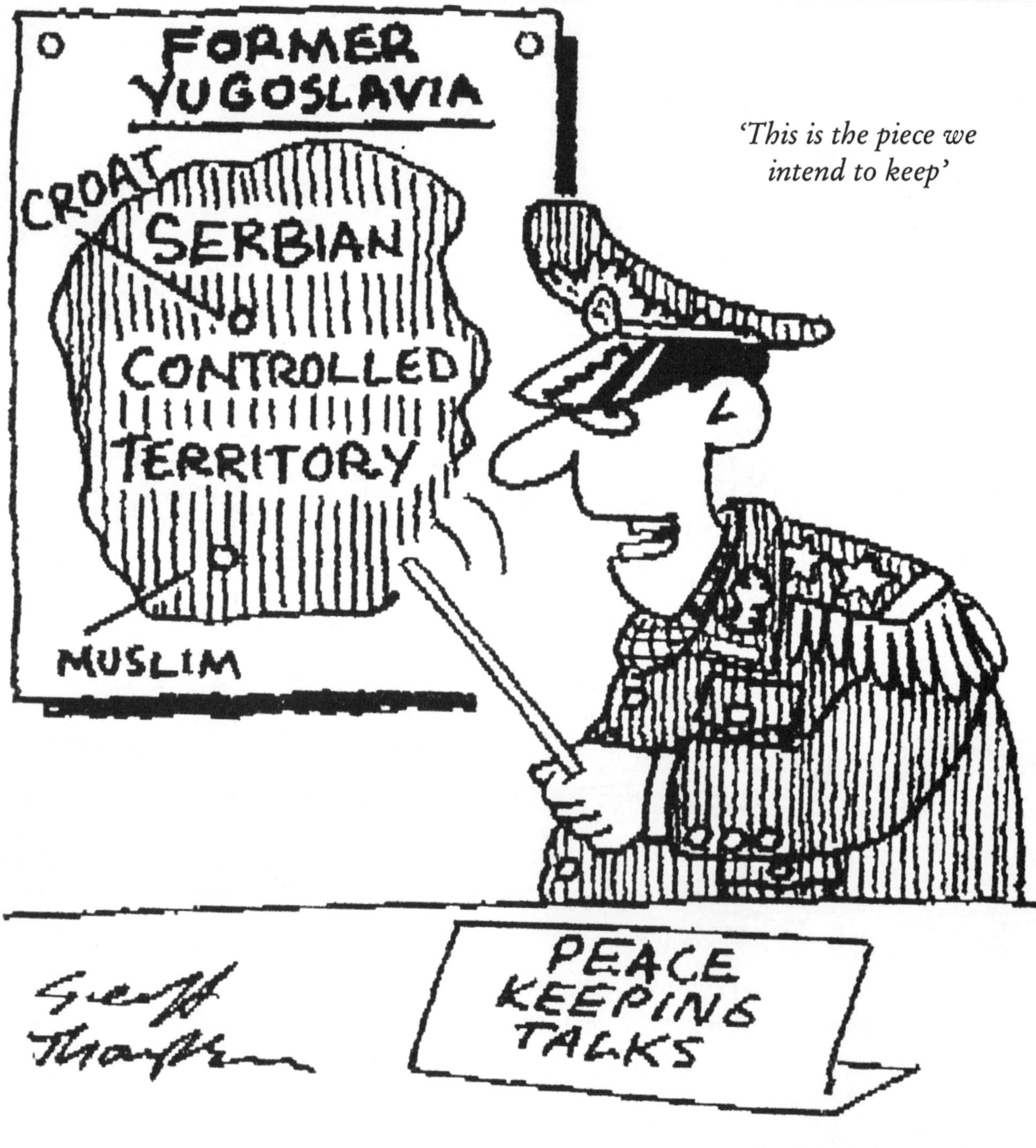
FORMER YUGOSLAVIA
CROAT
SERBIAN CONTROLLED TERRITORY
MUSLIM
PEACE KEEPING TALKS

'This is the piece we intend to keep'

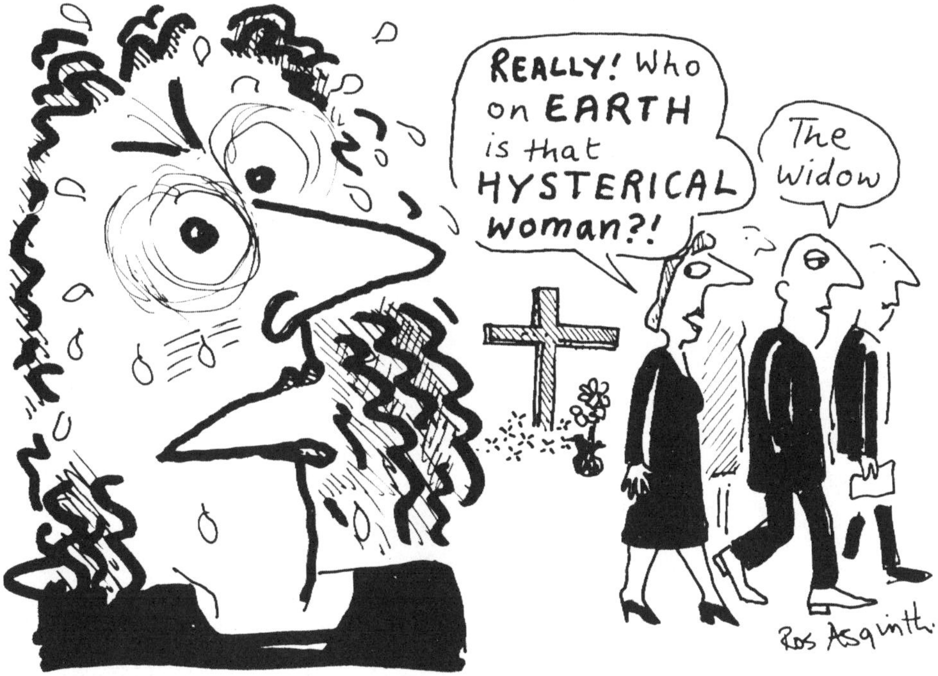
REALLY! Who on EARTH is that HYSTERICAL woman?!
The widow
Ros Asquith

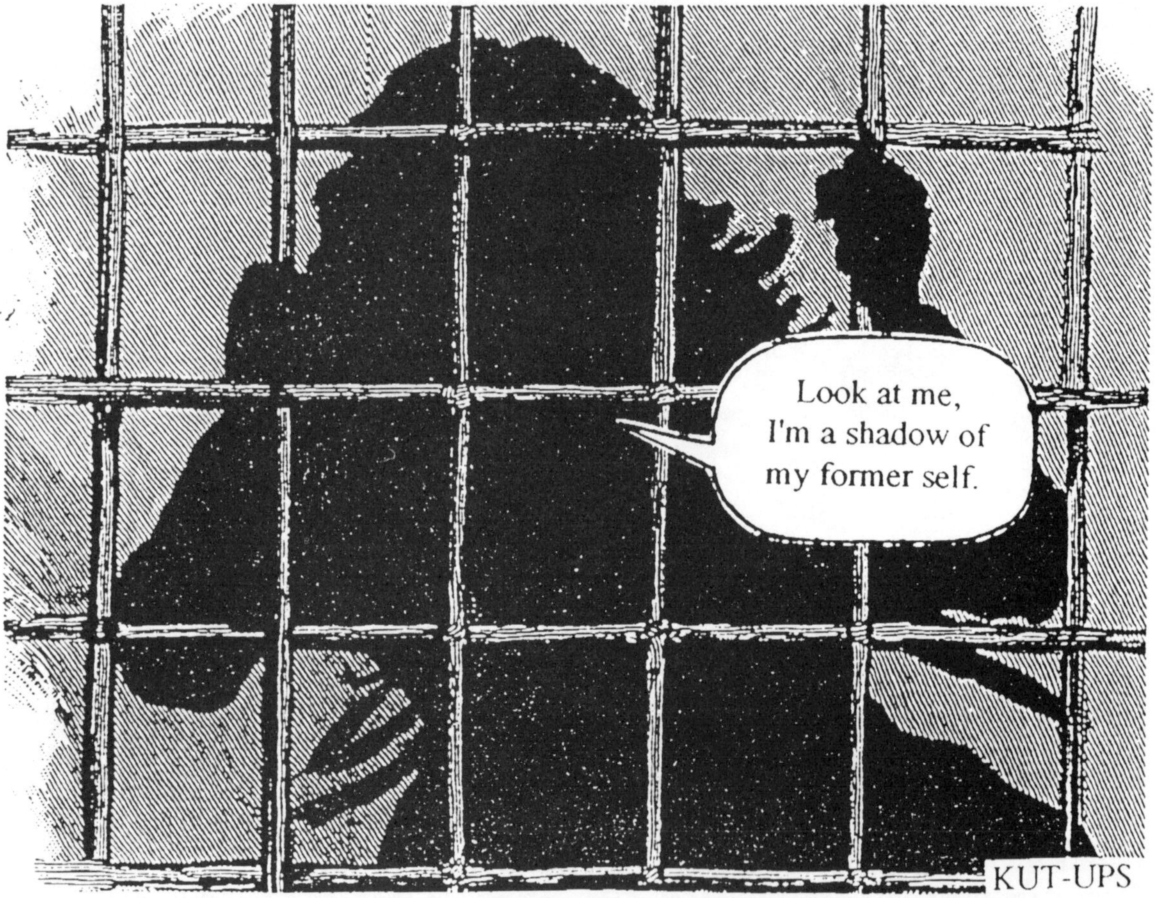
Look at me, I'm a shadow of my former self.
KUT-UPS

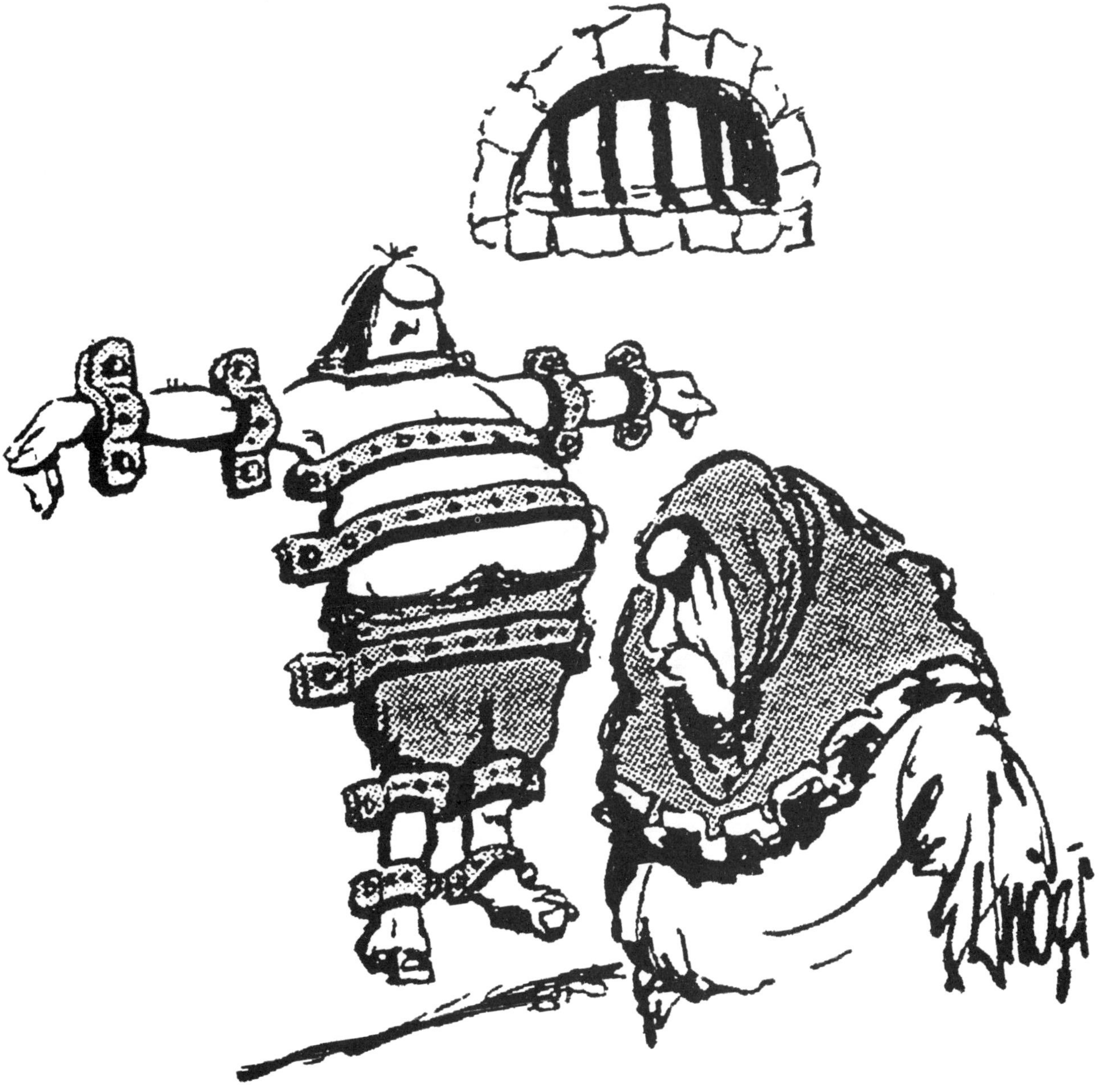

'What are my chances of time off for good behaviour?'

Well I want to be a Lesbian
Thats not a career
Well its bloody hard work in THIS COUNTRY.

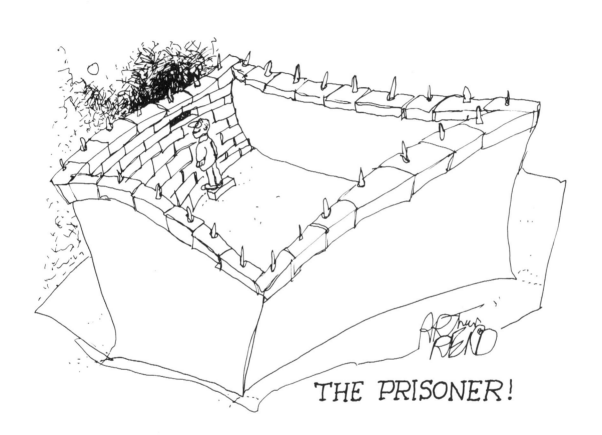

THE PRISONER!

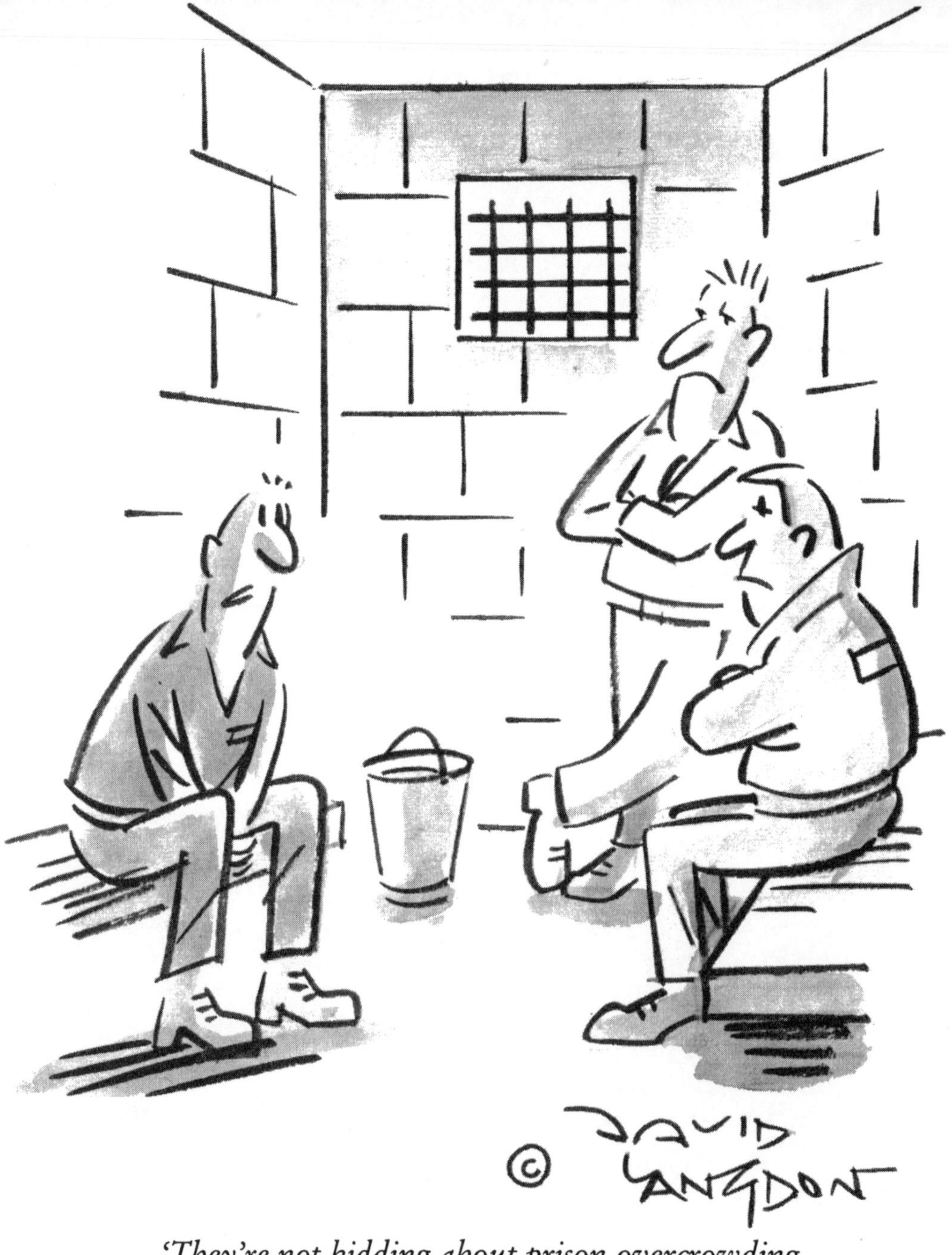
© DAVID LANGDON

'They're not kidding about prison overcrowding if they reckon this is solitary confinement'

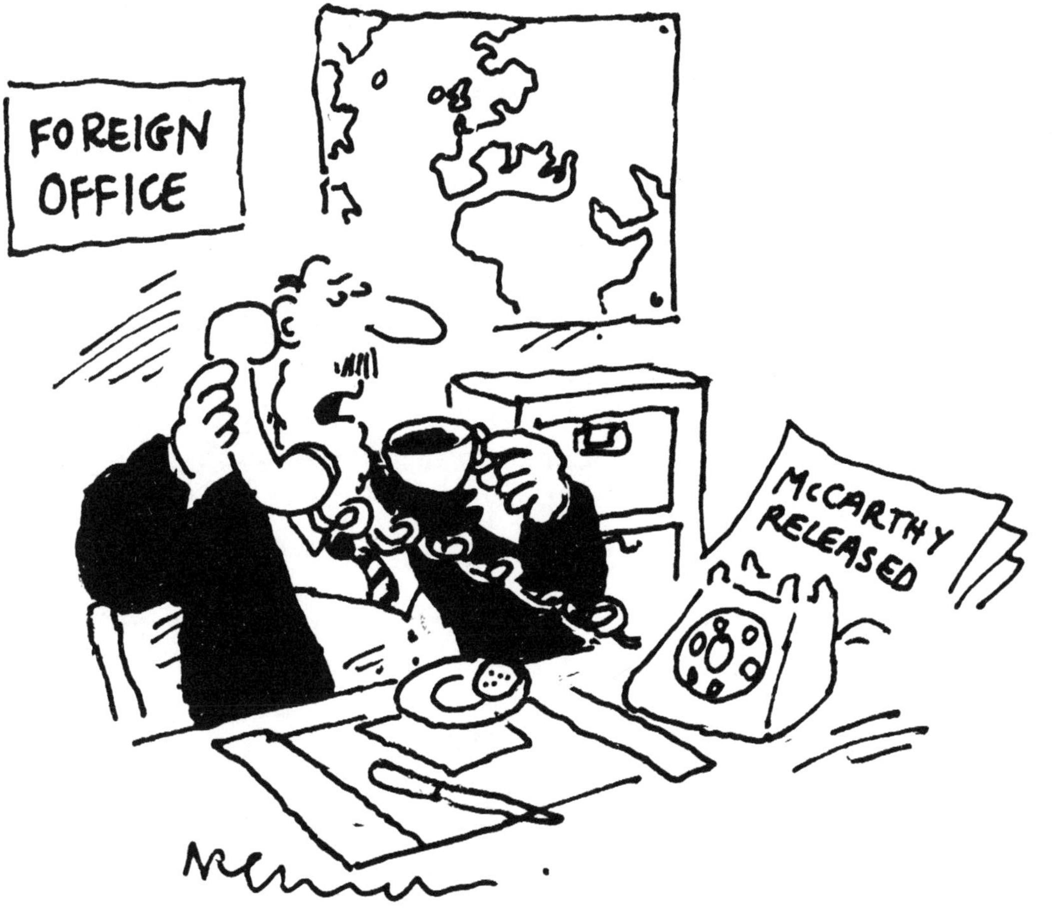
FOREIGN OFFICE
McCARTHY RELEASED

'Could we have done more? I'll get back to you in five years'

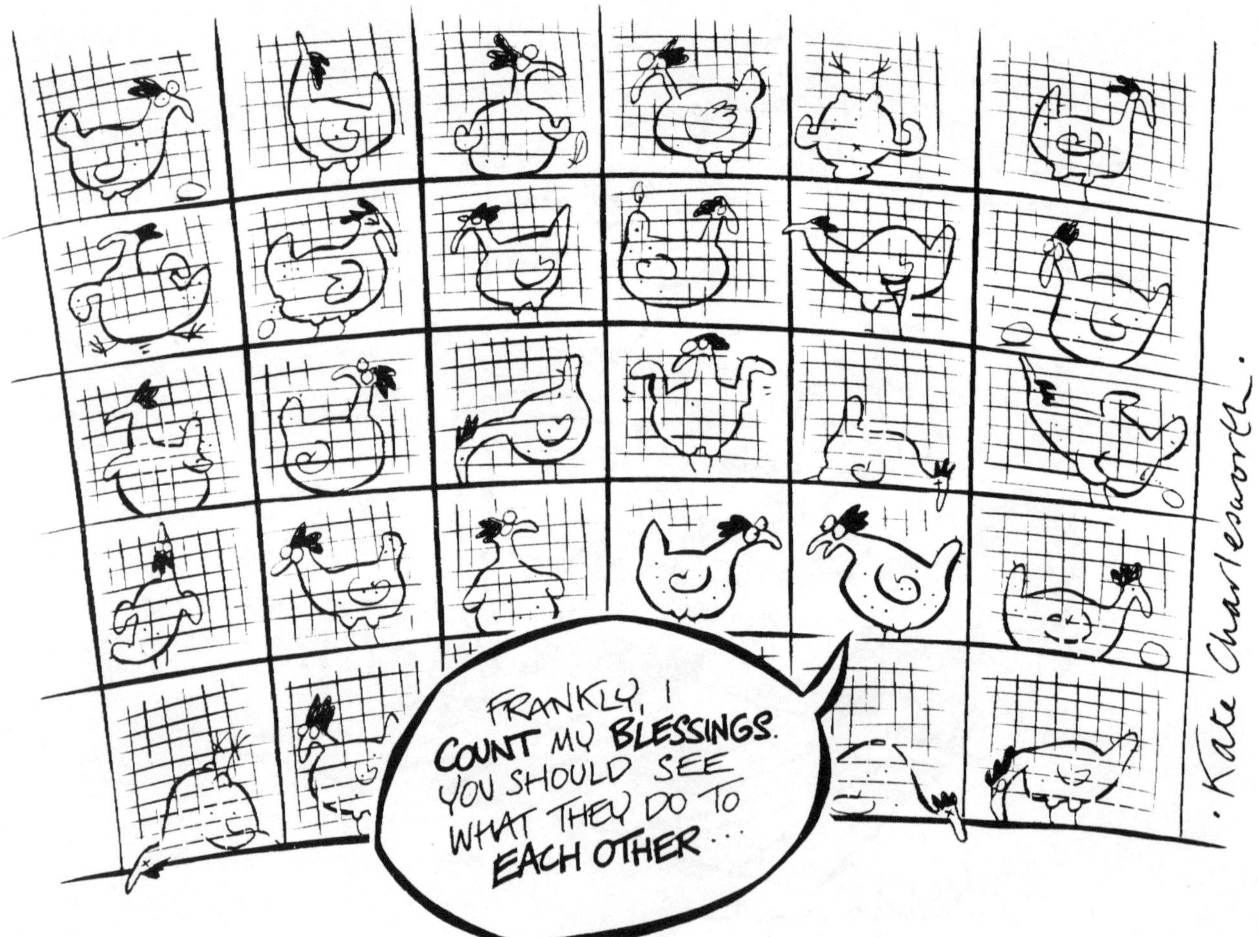
FRANKLY, I COUNT MY BLESSINGS. YOU SHOULD SEE WHAT THEY DO TO EACH OTHER...
Kate Charlesworth

Worthless pursuits No. 54. Experimenting with animals

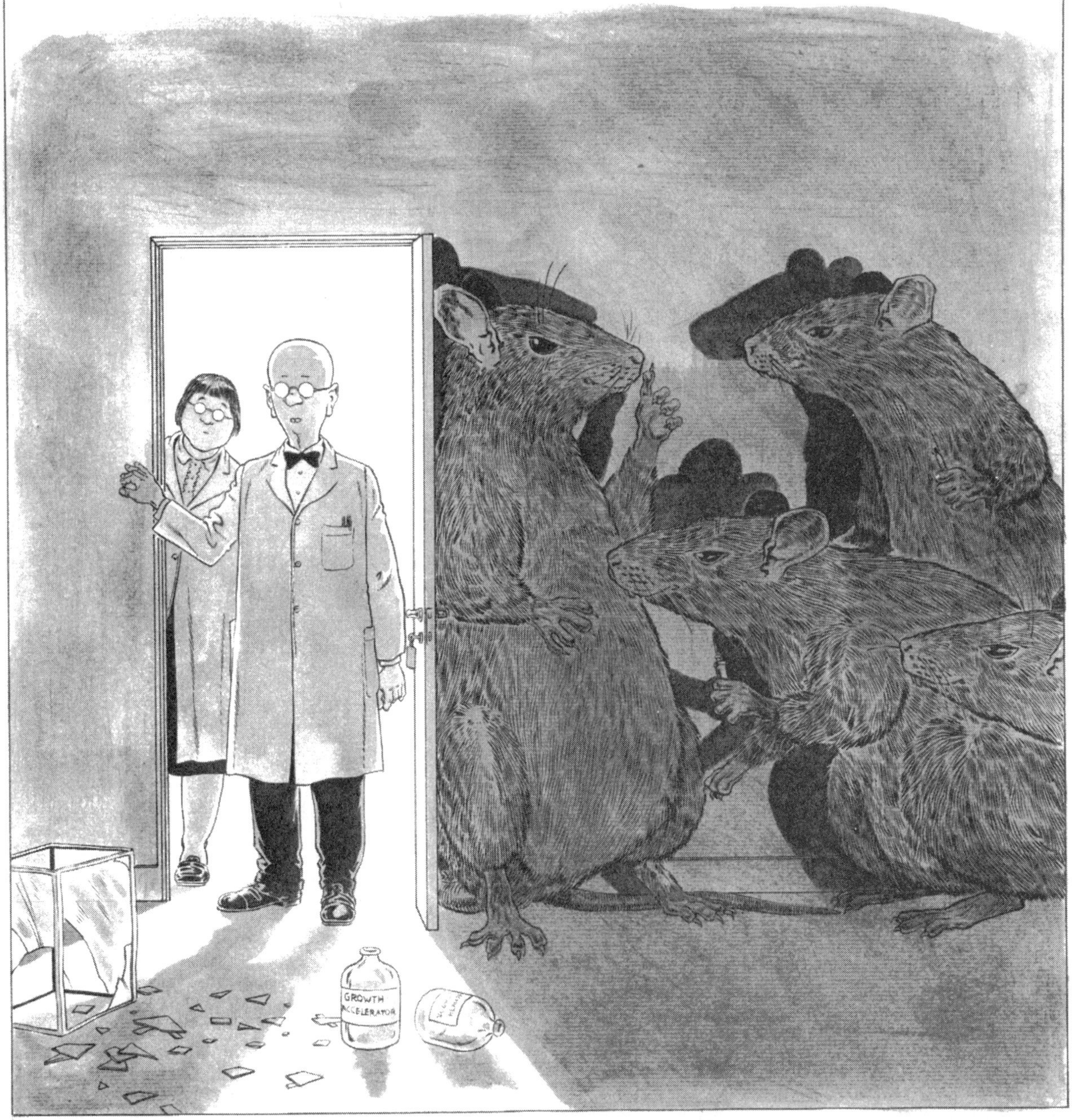
GROWTH ACCELERATOR

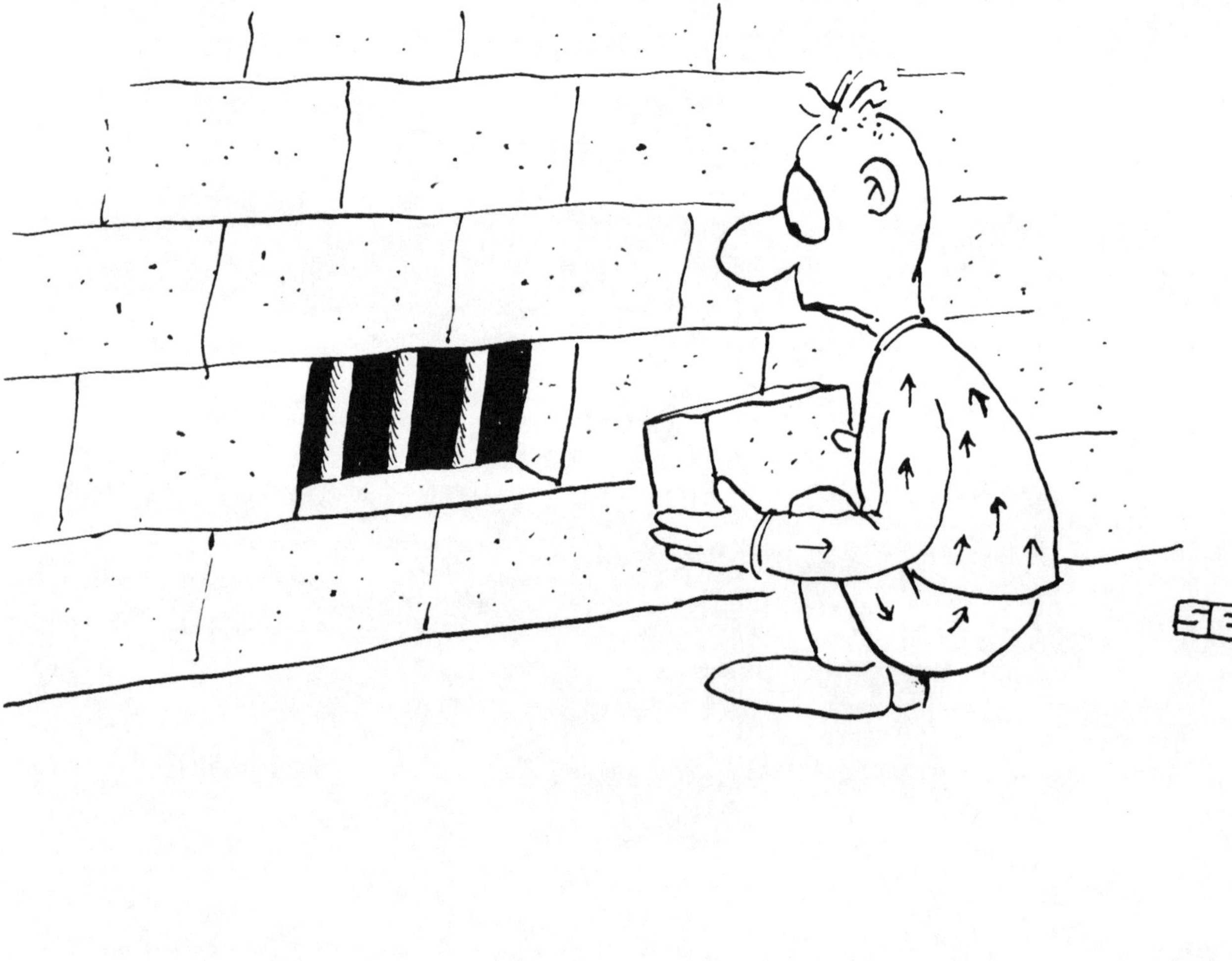

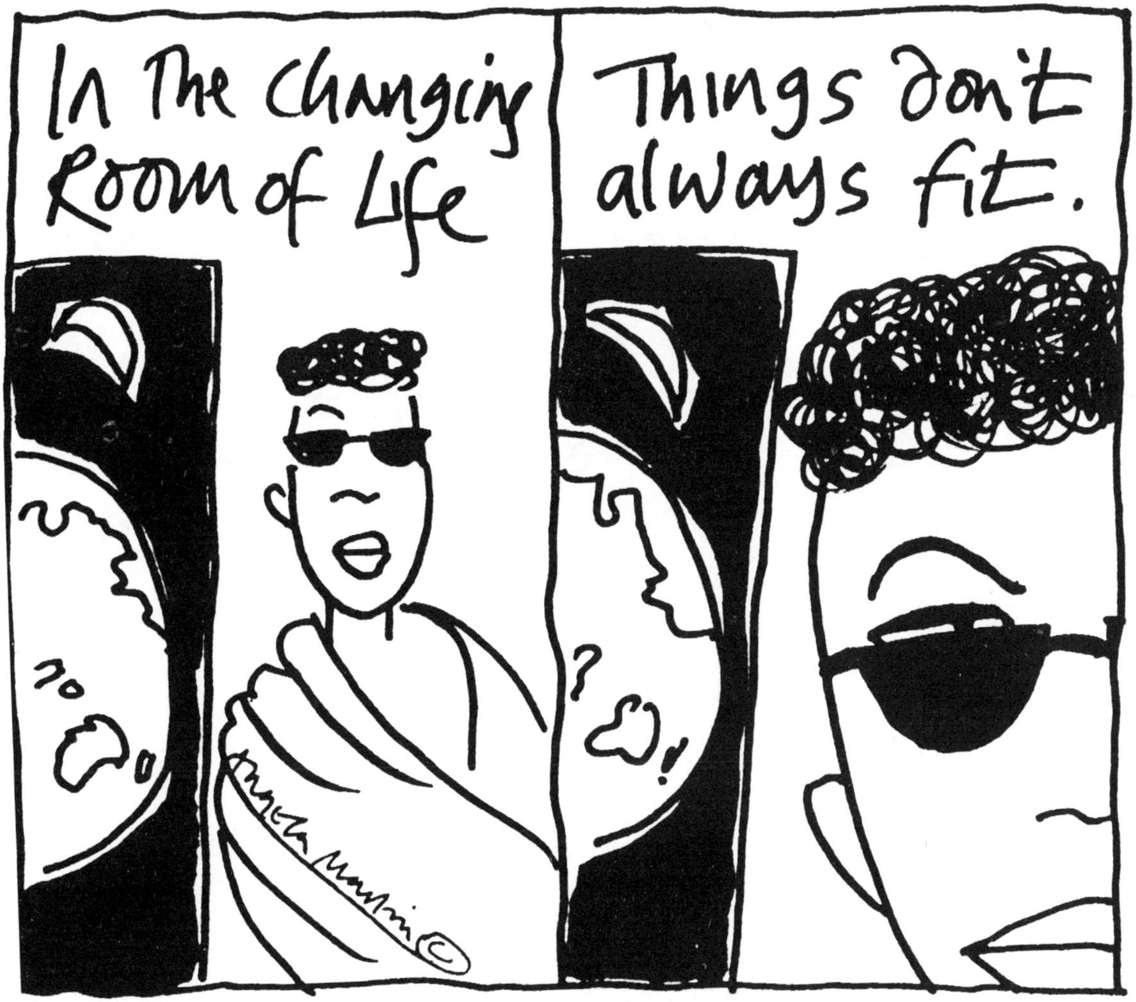
In The Changing Room of Life
Things don't always fit.

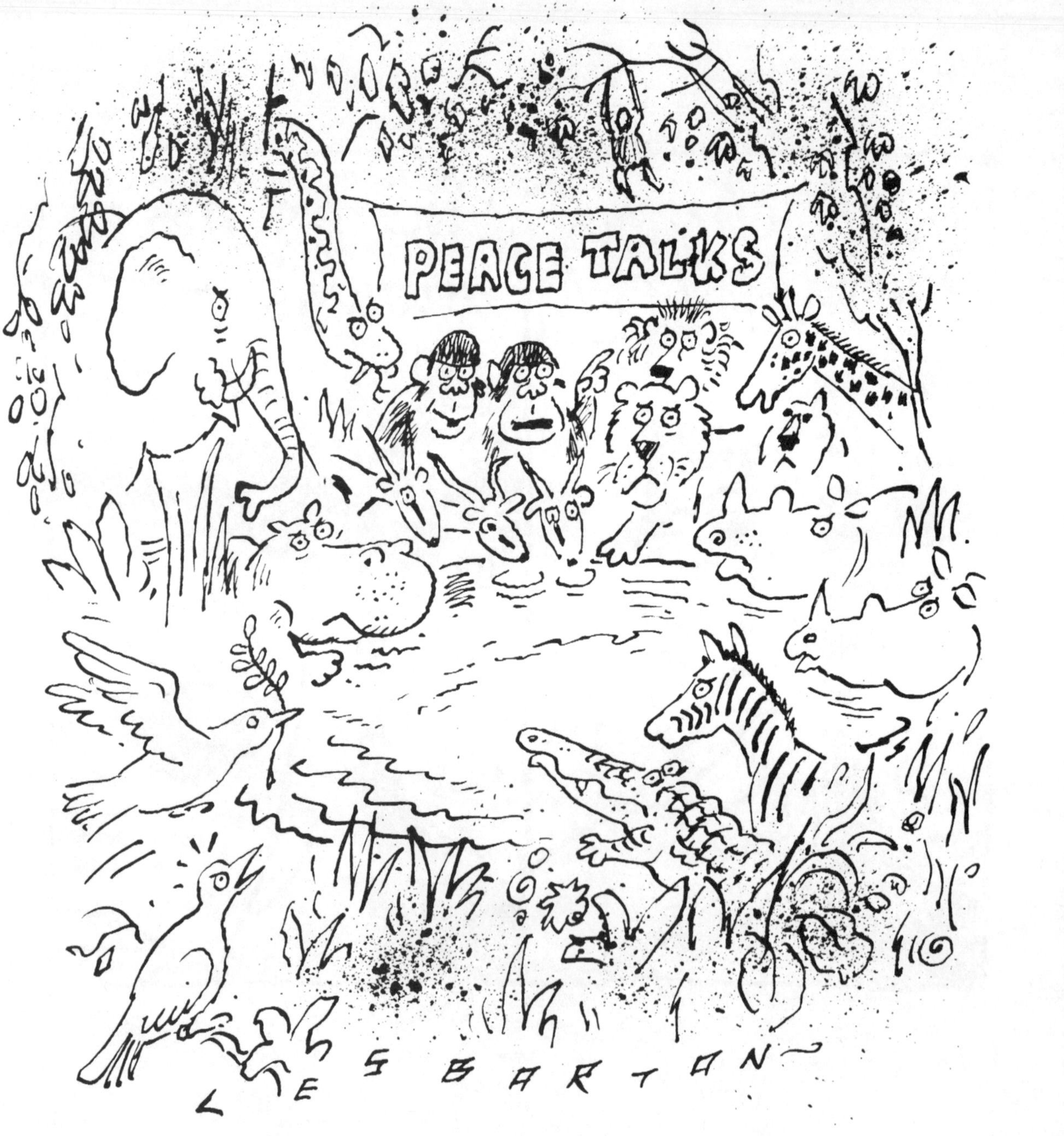
PEACE TALKS
LES BARTON

'It's a jungle out there'

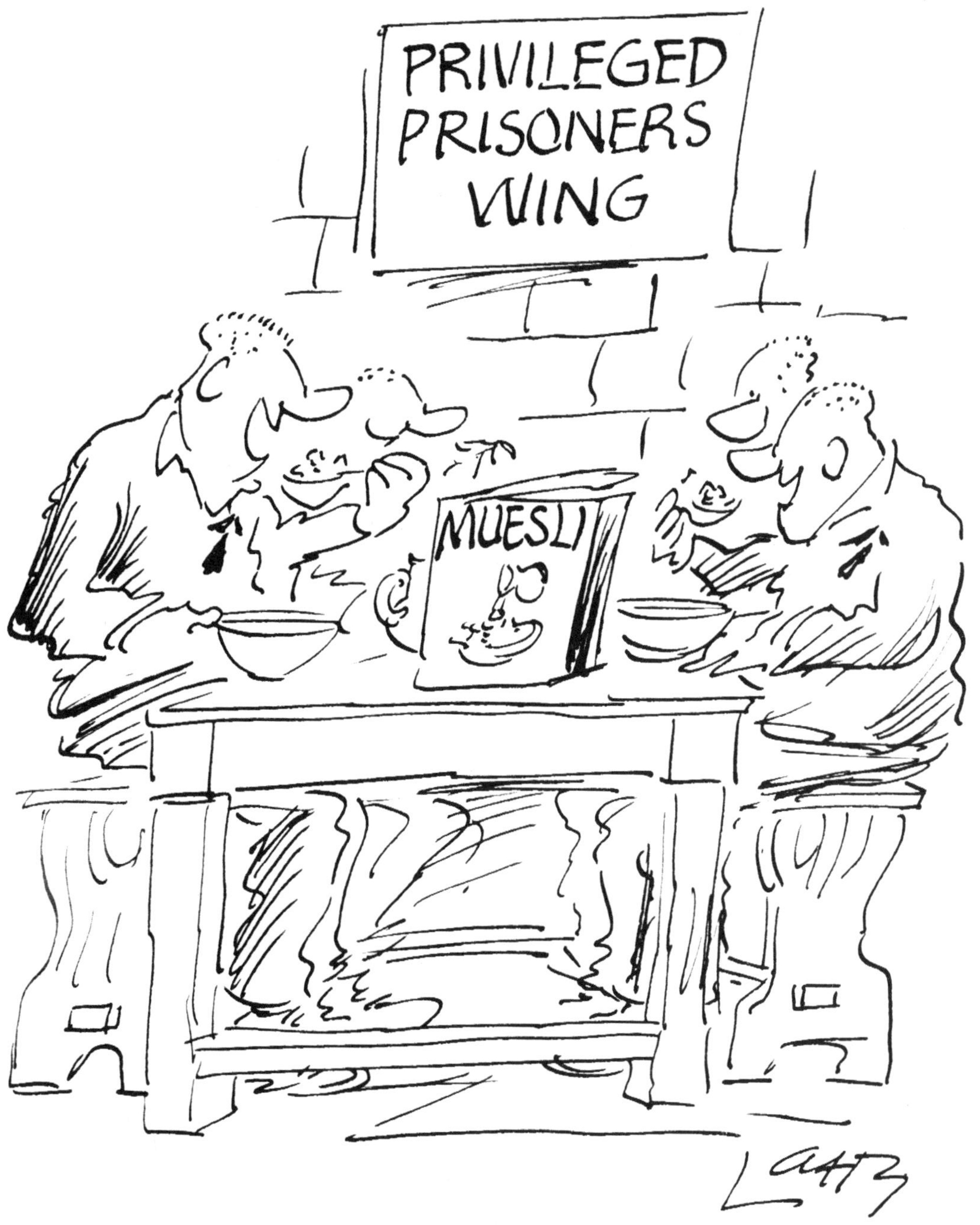
PRIVILEGED PRISONERS WING
MUESLI

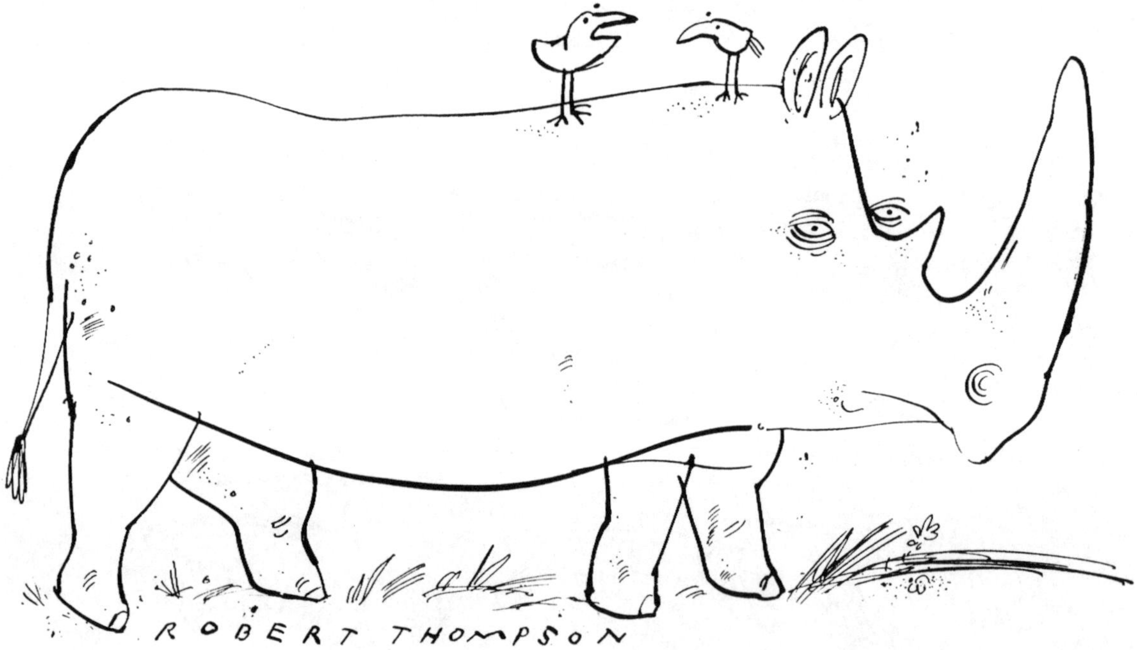
ROBERT THOMPSON

'He's not a bad bloke to work for. So long as you don't get up his nose'

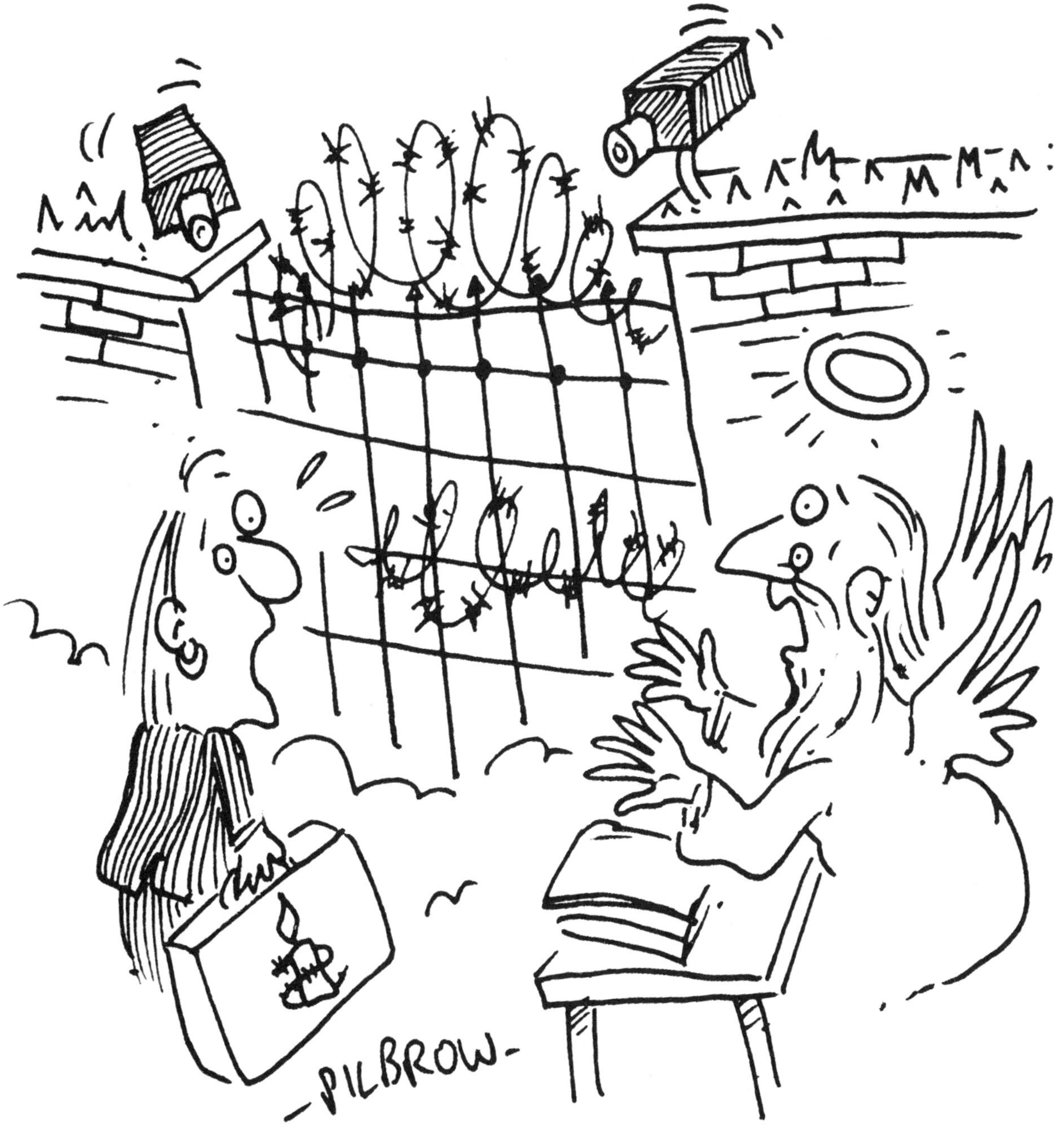
PILBROW

'It's been like this ever since somebody knicked the Pearly Gates'

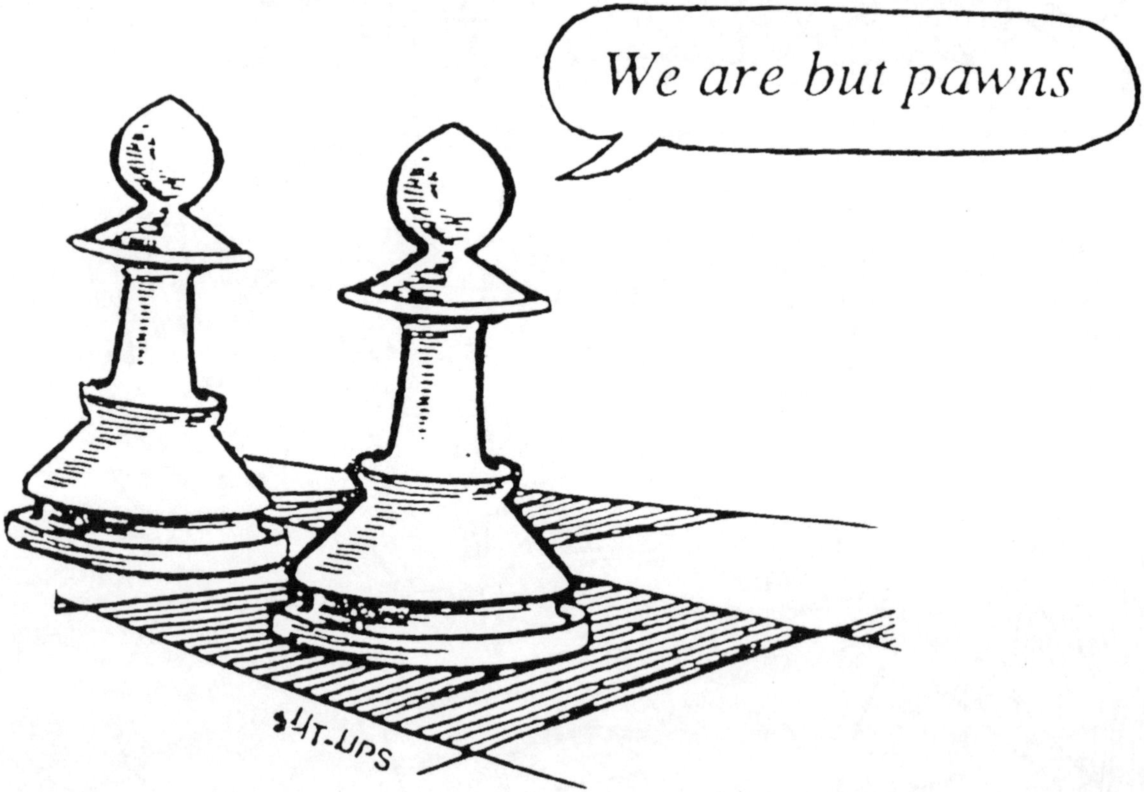
We are but pawns

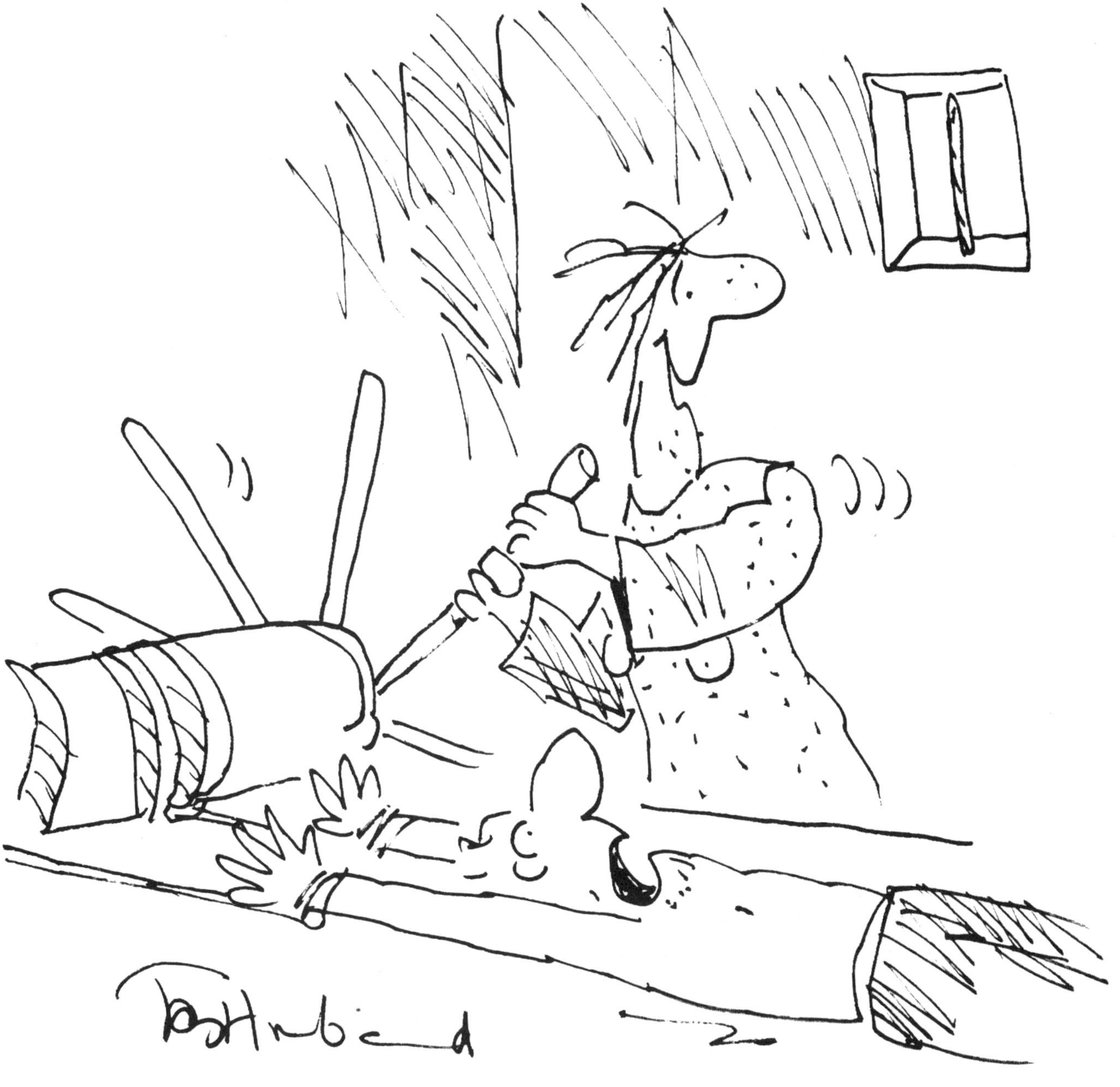

'Mum .. Dad .. Count Norbert says he'll marry me'

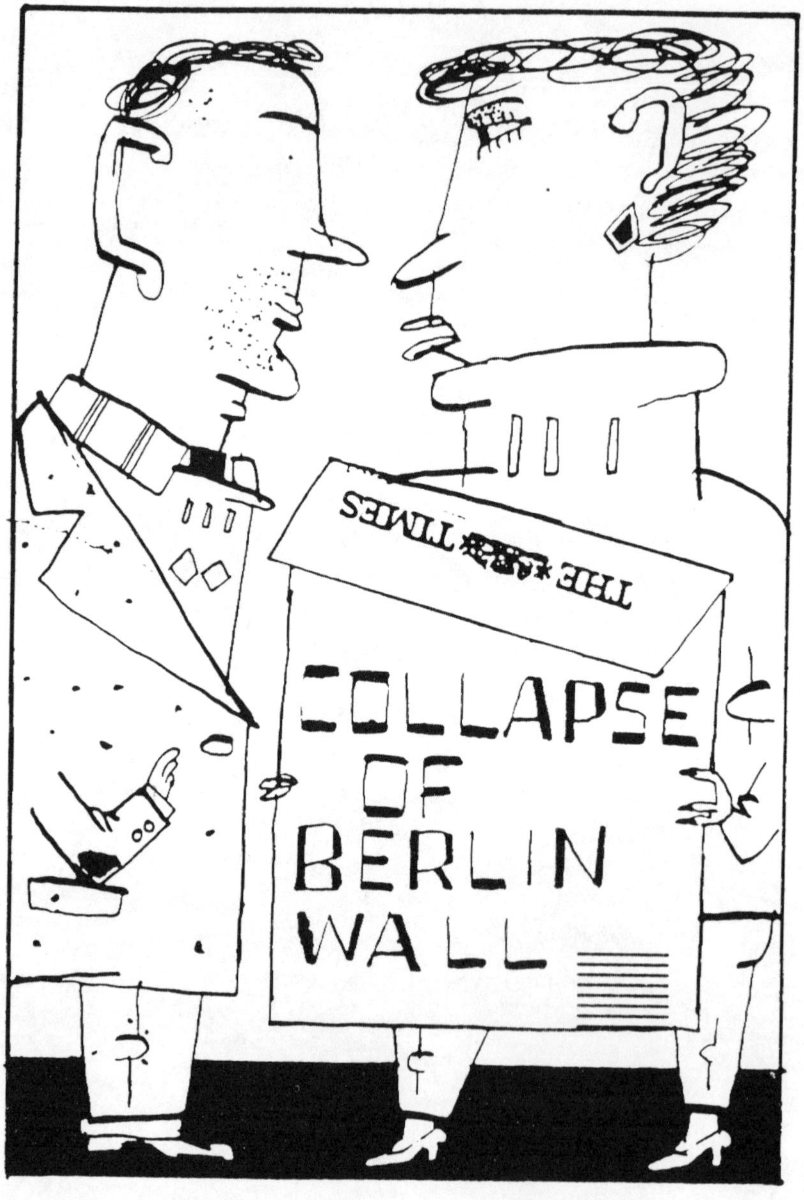
THE
TIMES
COLLAPSE OF BERLIN WALL

'Only 28 years – they must have used the same builder who did our loft conversion'

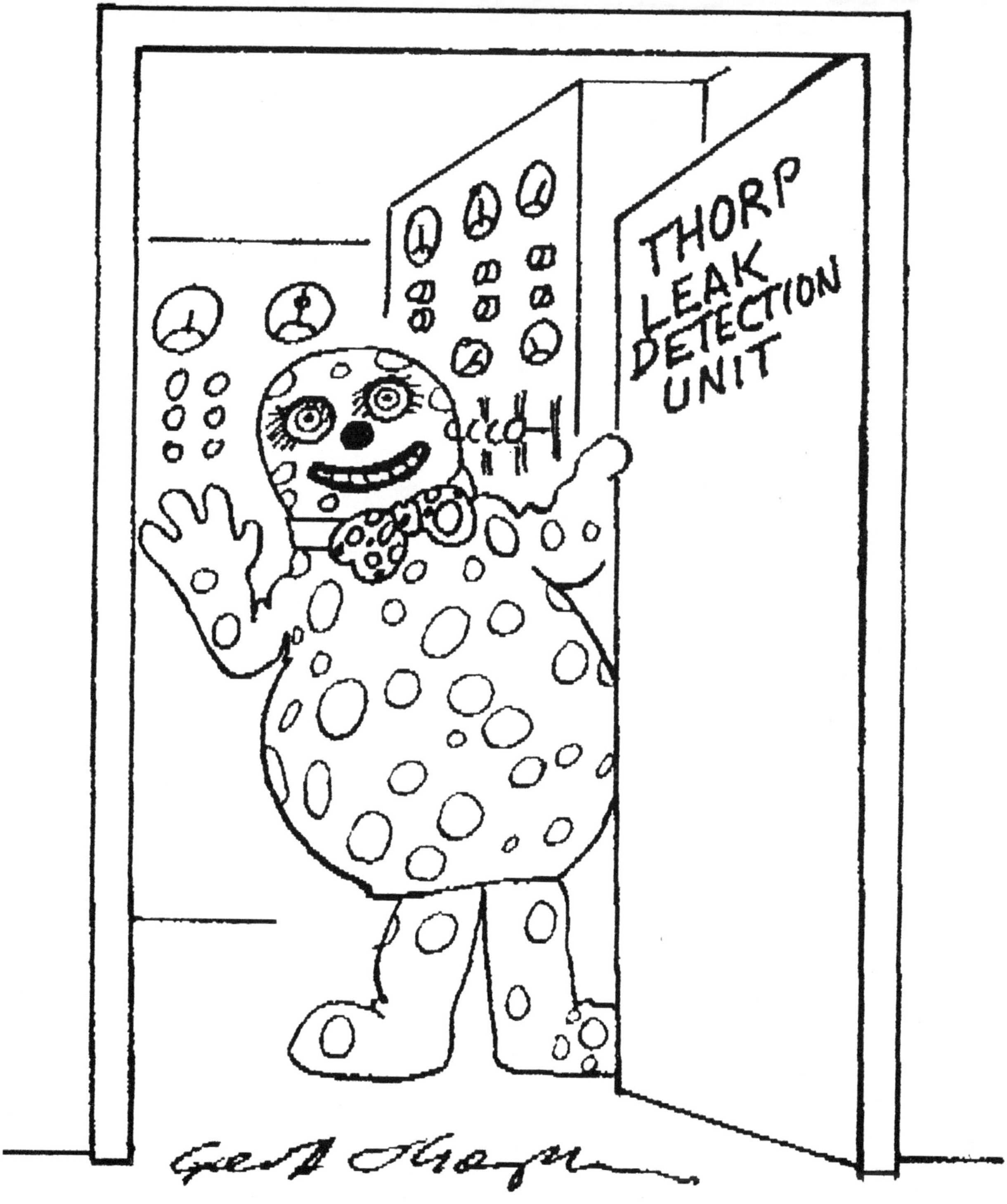
THORP
LEAK
DETECTION
UNIT

I don't see why they shouldn't play with guns. After all, we did.
Ros Asquith.

1950s...
CONSCIENCIOUS OBJECTION!

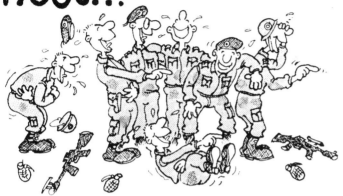

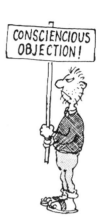

1990s...

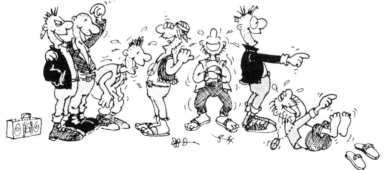

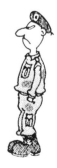

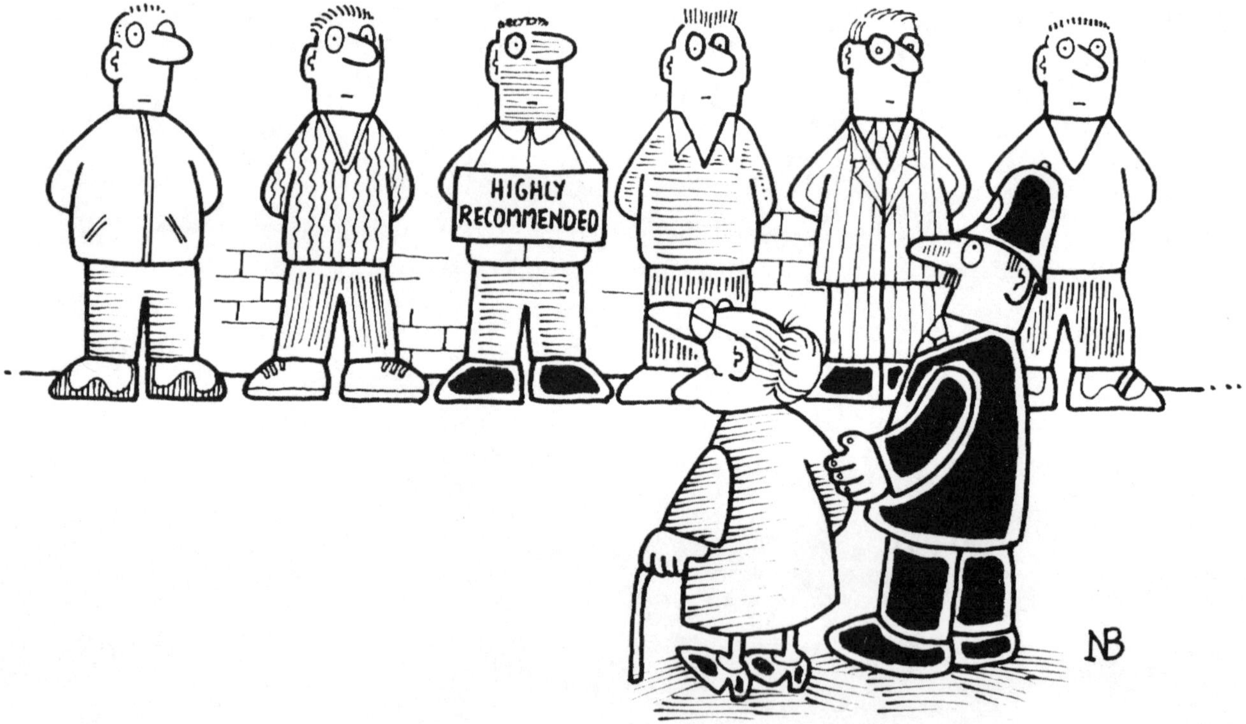
HIGHLY RECOMMENDED
NB

Well whaddya Know! I ain't been in therapy for five years either!
Ros Asquith

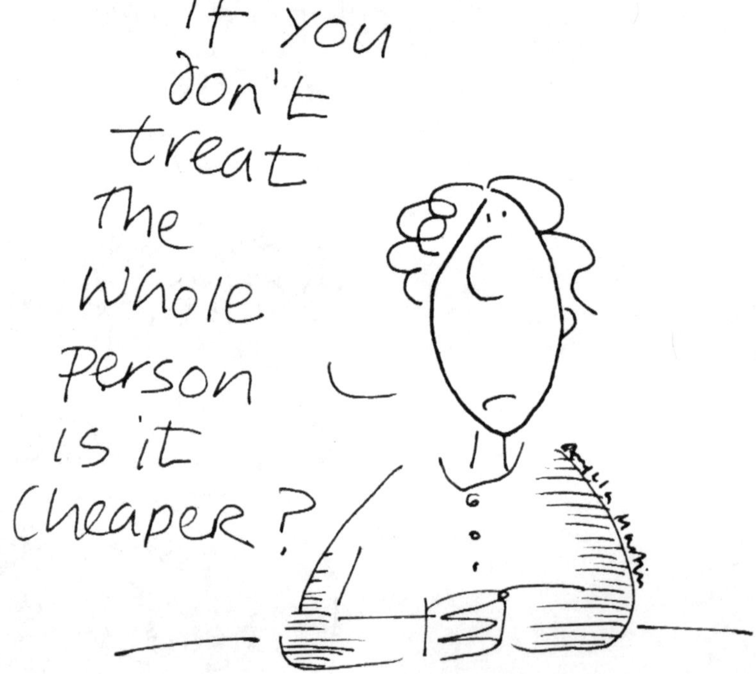
If you don't treat the whole person is it cheaper?

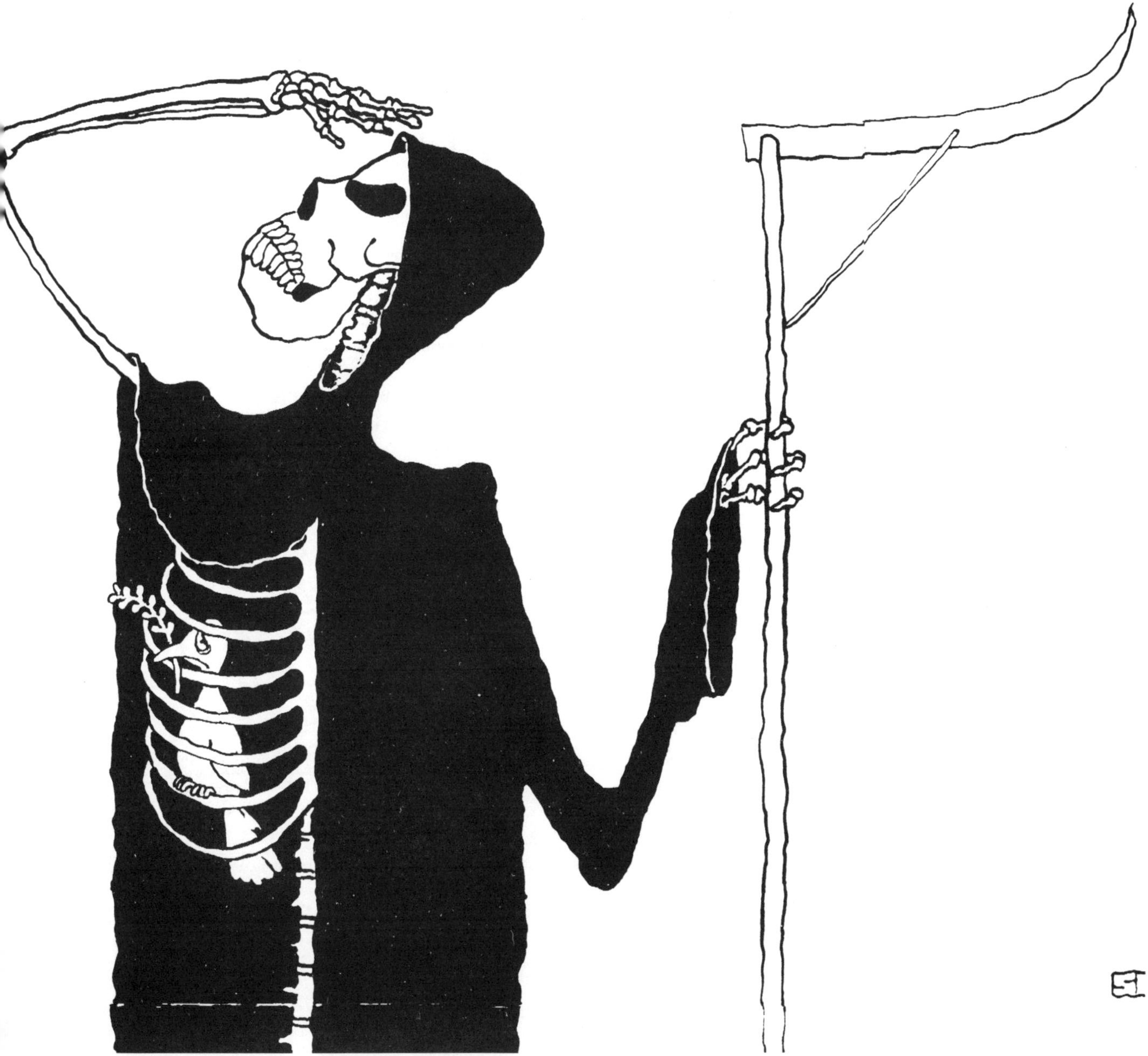

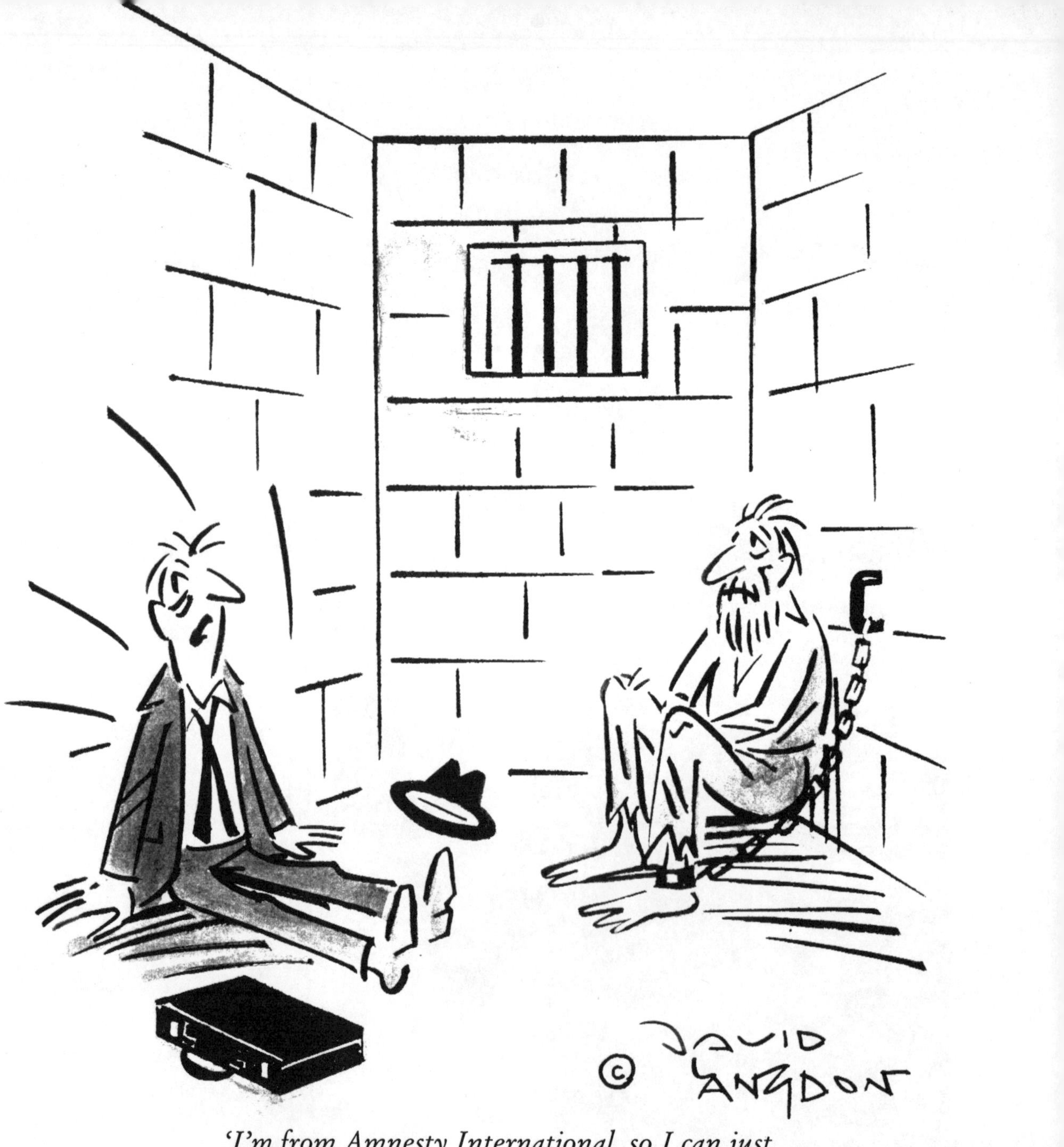
© DAVID LANGDON

'I'm from Amnesty International, so I can just imagine how they must be treating <u>*YOU*</u> *'*

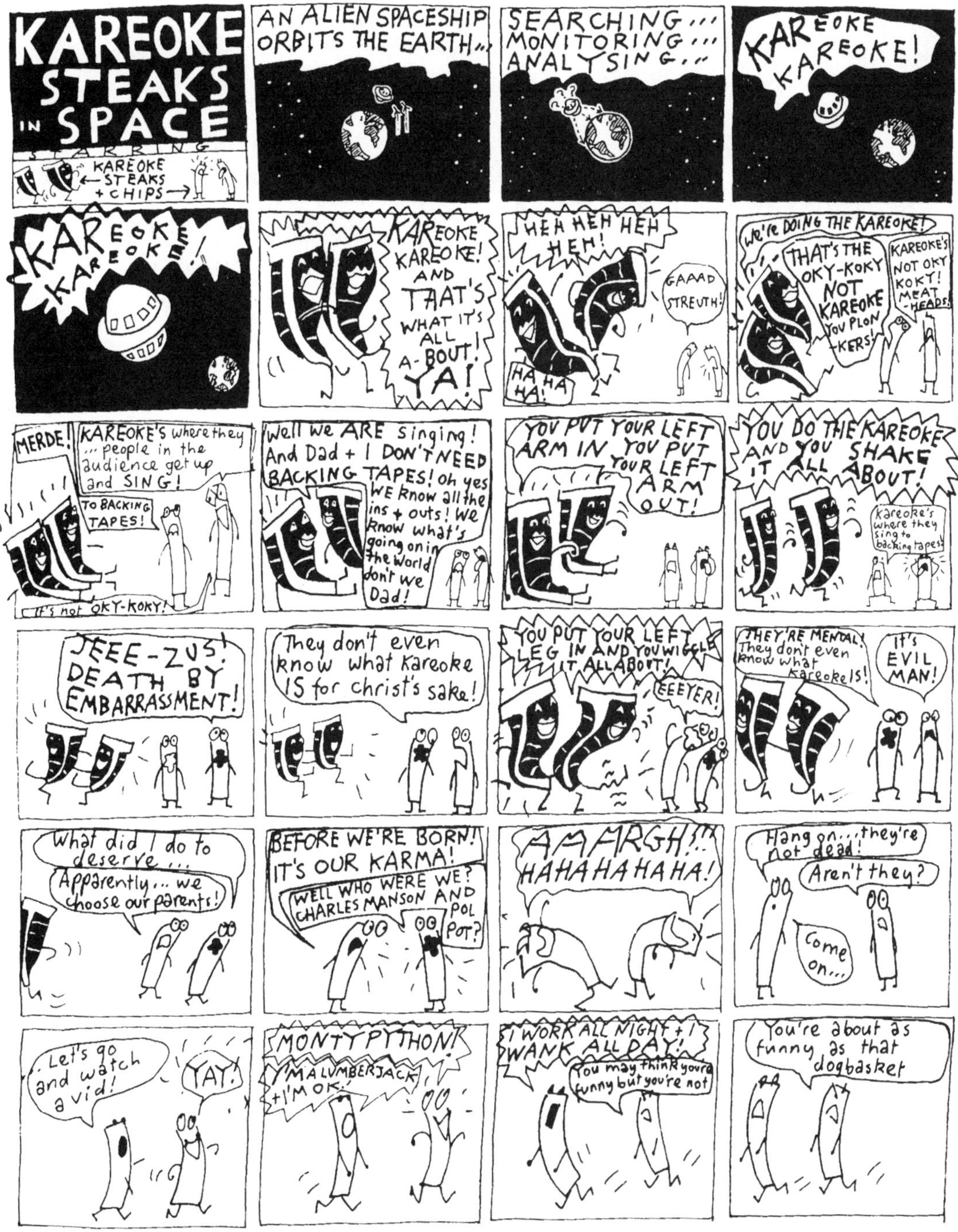
KAREOKE STEAKS IN SPACE
STARRING
KAREOKE STEAKS + CHIPS
AN ALIEN SPACESHIP ORBITS THE EARTH...
SEARCHING... MONITORING... ANALYSING...
KAREOKE KAREOKE!
KAREOKE KAREOKE!
KAREOKE KAREOKE! AND THAT'S WHAT IT'S ALL A-BOUT! YA!
HEH HEH HEH HEH!
GAAAD STREUTH!
HA HA HA!
We're DOING THE KAREOKE!
THAT'S THE OKY-KOKY NOT KAREOKE YOU PLONKERS!
KAREOKE'S NOT OKY KOKY! MEAT-HEADS!
MERDE!
KAREOKE's where they ... people in the audience get up and SING!
TO BACKING TAPES!
IT'S not OKY-KOKY!
Well we ARE singing! And Dad + I DON'T NEED BACKING TAPES! oh yes WE know all the ins + outs! We know what's going on in the World don't we Dad!
YOU PUT YOUR LEFT ARM IN YOU PUT YOUR LEFT ARM OUT!
YOU DO THE KAREOKE AND YOU SHAKE IT ALL ABOUT!
kareoke's where they sing to backing tapes!
JEEE-ZUS! DEATH BY EMBARRASSMENT!
They don't even know what kareoke IS for christ's sake!
YOU PUT YOUR LEFT LEG IN AND YOU WIGGLE IT ALL ABOUT!
EEEYER!
THEY'RE MENTAL! They don't even know what kareoke IS!
It's EVIL MAN!
What did I do to deserve...
Apparently... we choose our parents!
BEFORE WE'RE BORN! IT'S OUR KARMA!
WELL WHO WERE WE? CHARLES MANSON AND POL POT?
AAAARGH!!! HAHAHAHAHA!
Hang on... they're not dead!
Aren't they?
Come on...
Let's go and watch a vid!
YAY!
MONTY PYTHON!
I'M A LUMBERJACK + I'M OK!
I WORK ALL NIGHT + I WANK ALL DAY!
You may think you're funny but you're not
You're about as funny as that dogbasket

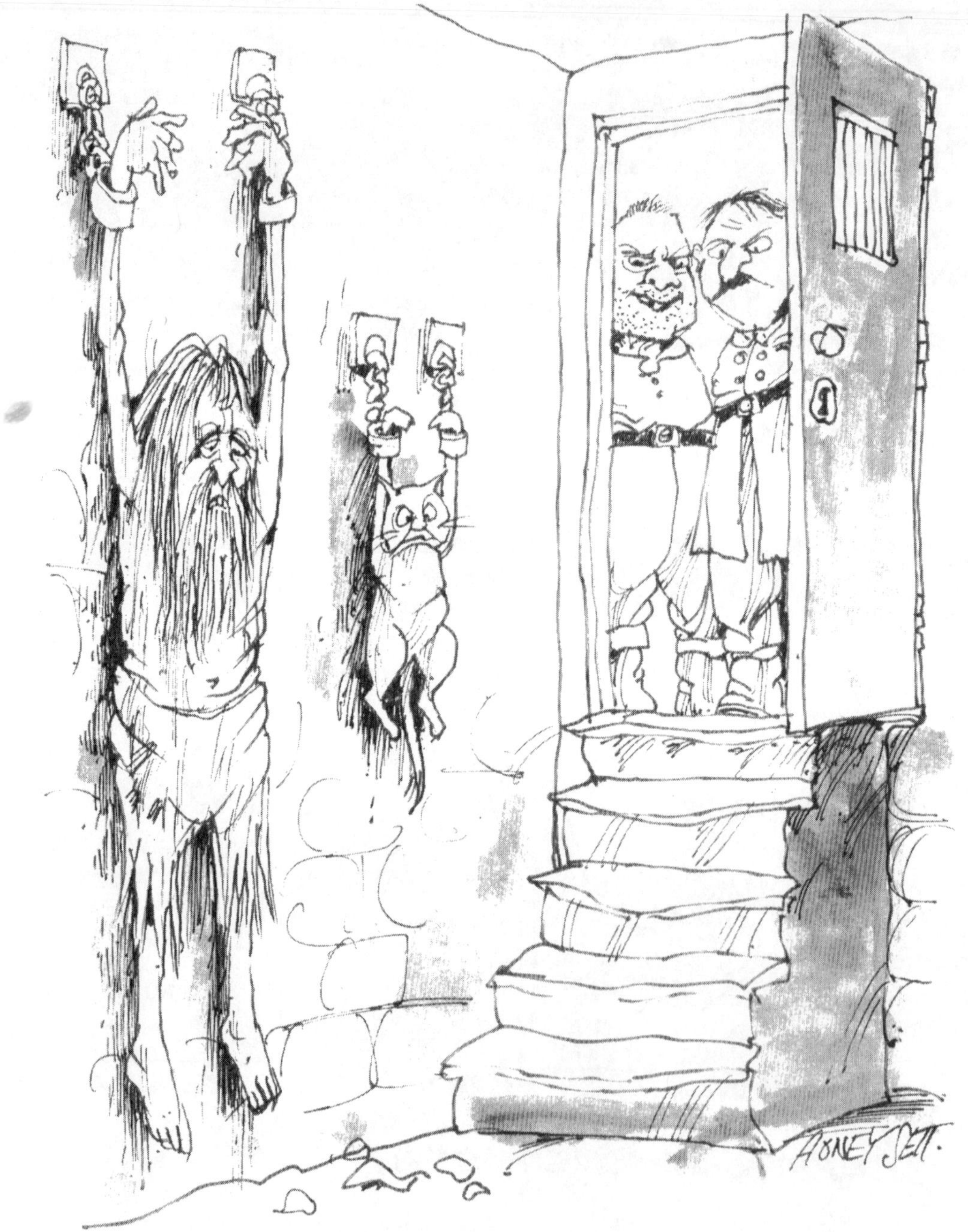
HONEYSETT.

'As a humanitarian gesture we let them keep pets'

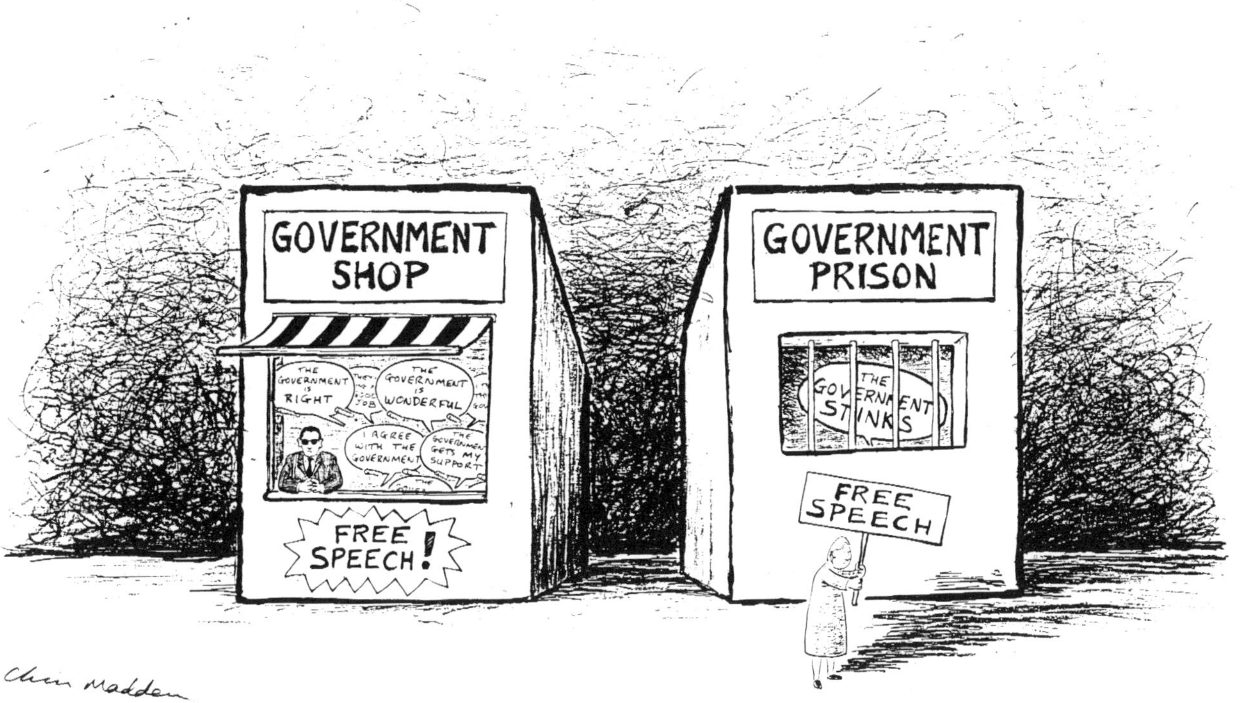
GOVERNMENT SHOP
THE GOVERNMENT IS RIGHT
THE GOVERNMENT IS WONDERFUL
I AGREE WITH THE GOVERNMENT
THE GOVERNMENT GETS MY SUPPORT
FREE SPEECH!
GOVERNMENT PRISON
THE GOVERNMENT STINKS
FREE SPEECH
Chris Madden

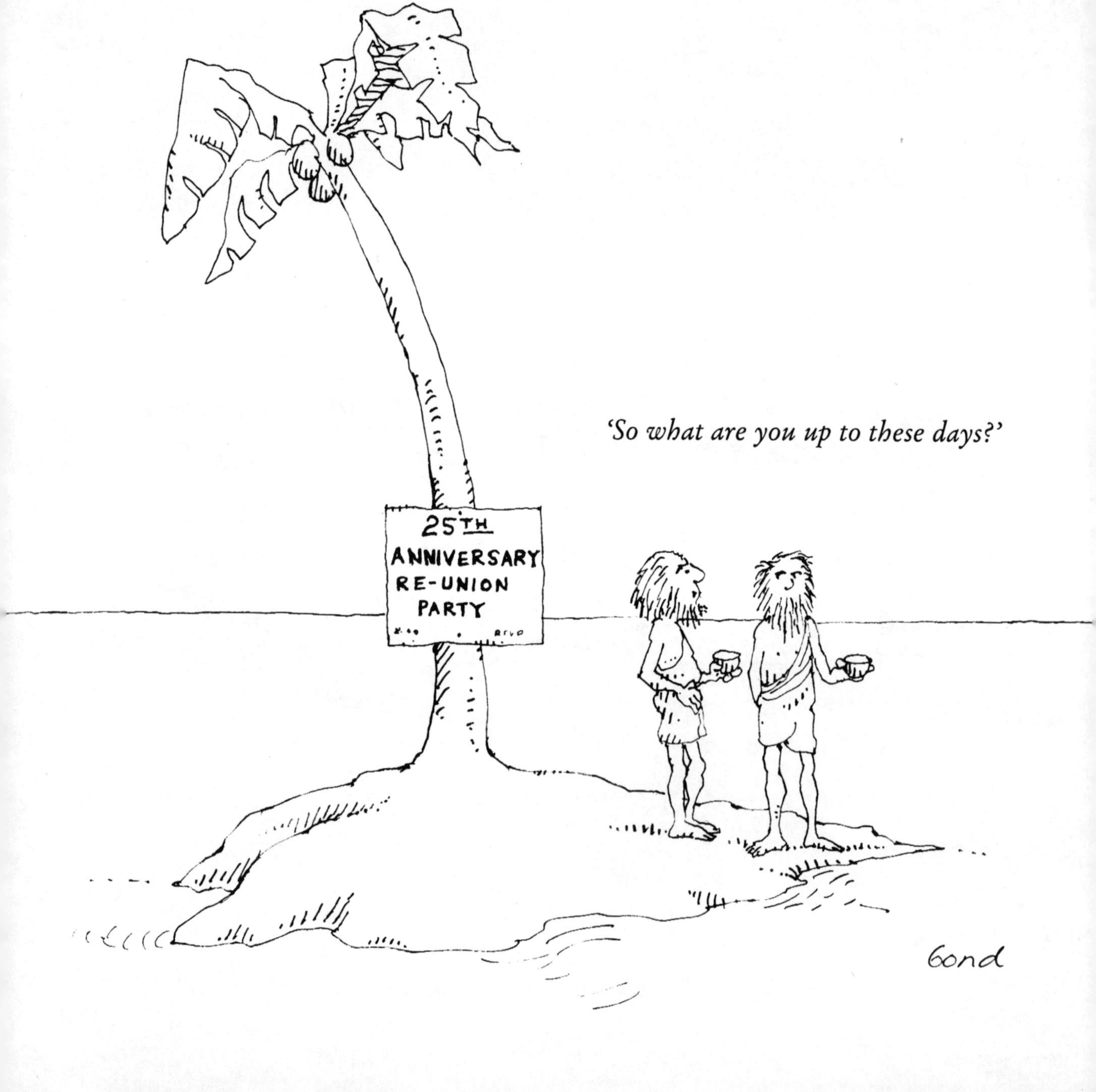
25TH
ANNIVERSARY
RE-UNION
PARTY
Gond

'So what are you up to these days?'

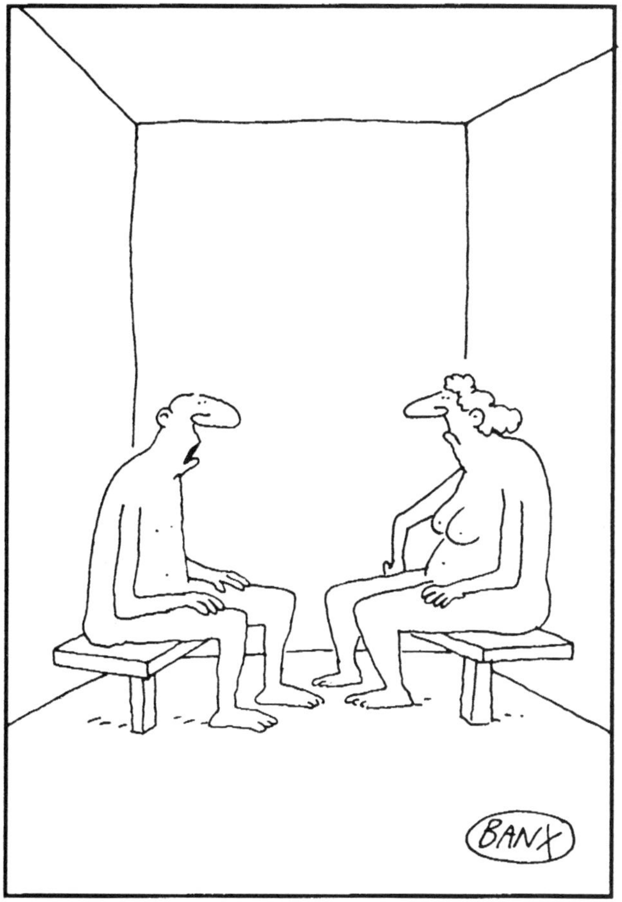
BANX

'Hell doesn't exist – this is purgatory'

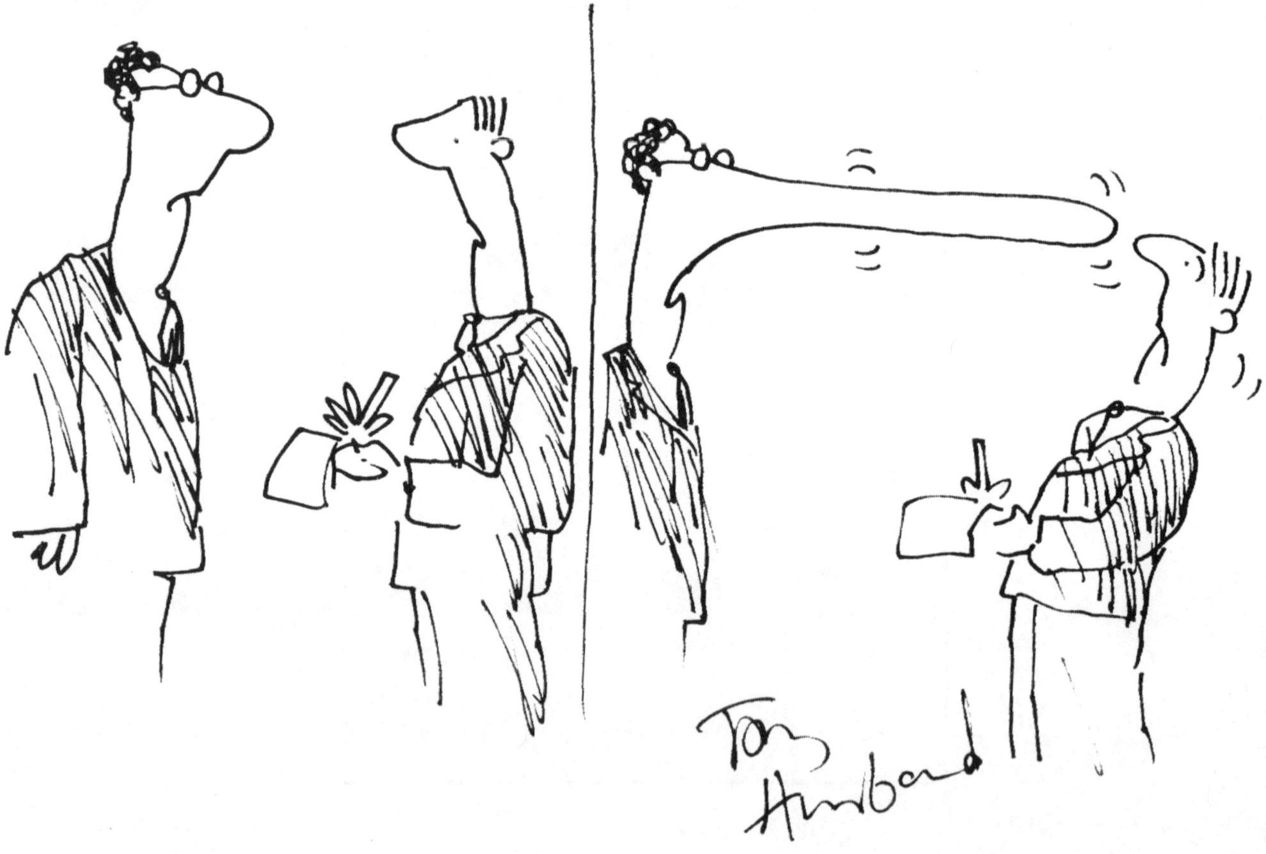

'So minister you deny any human rights violation in this country?'

'Of course I do emphatically'

*Soldier placing a wreath at the tomb
of the unknown prime minister*

you got to laugh

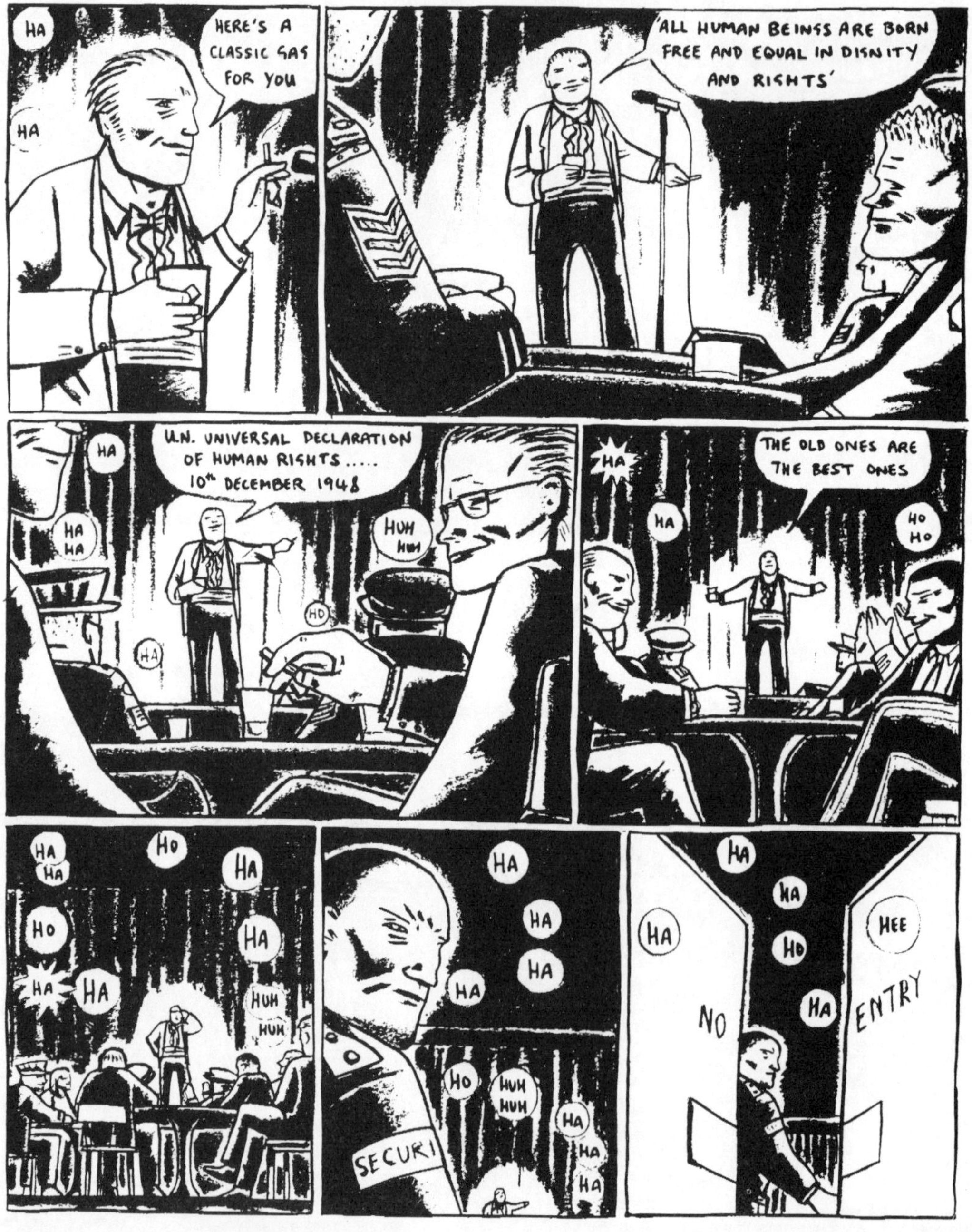
HA
HERE'S A CLASSIC GAG FOR YOU
HA
'ALL HUMAN BEINGS ARE BORN FREE AND EQUAL IN DIGNITY AND RIGHTS'
HA
U.N. UNIVERSAL DECLARATION OF HUMAN RIGHTS..... 10th DECEMBER 1948
HA HA
HUH HUH
HO
HA
HA
THE OLD ONES ARE THE BEST ONES
HA
HO HO
HA HA
HO
HA
HO
HA
HA
HA
HUH HUH
HA
HA
HA
HA
HO
HUH HUH
HA
HA
HA
SECURI
HA
HA
HA
HEE
HO
NO
HA
ENTRY

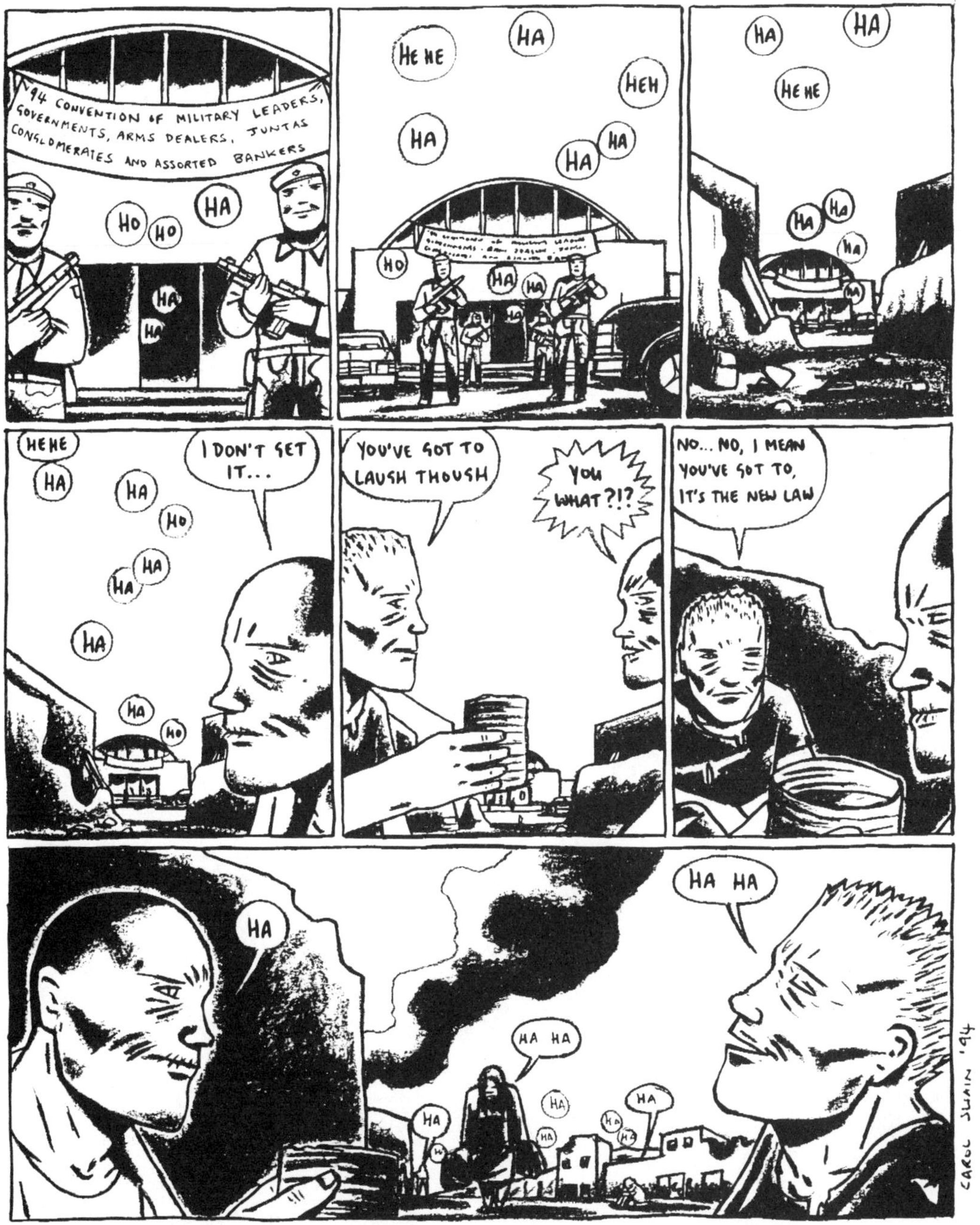
'94 CONVENTION OF MILITARY LEADERS, GOVERNMENTS, ARMS DEALERS, JUNTAS CONGLOMERATES AND ASSORTED BANKERS
HO
HO
HA
HA
HA
HE HE
HA
HEH
HA
HA
HA
HO
HA
HA
HA
HA
HE HE
HA
HA
HE HE
HA
HA
I DON'T GET IT...
HO
HA
HA
HA
HA
HO
YOU'VE GOT TO LAUGH THOUGH
YOU WHAT?!?
NO... NO, I MEAN YOU'VE GOT TO, IT'S THE NEW LAW
HA
HA HA
HA HA
HA
HA
HA
CAROL SWAIN '94

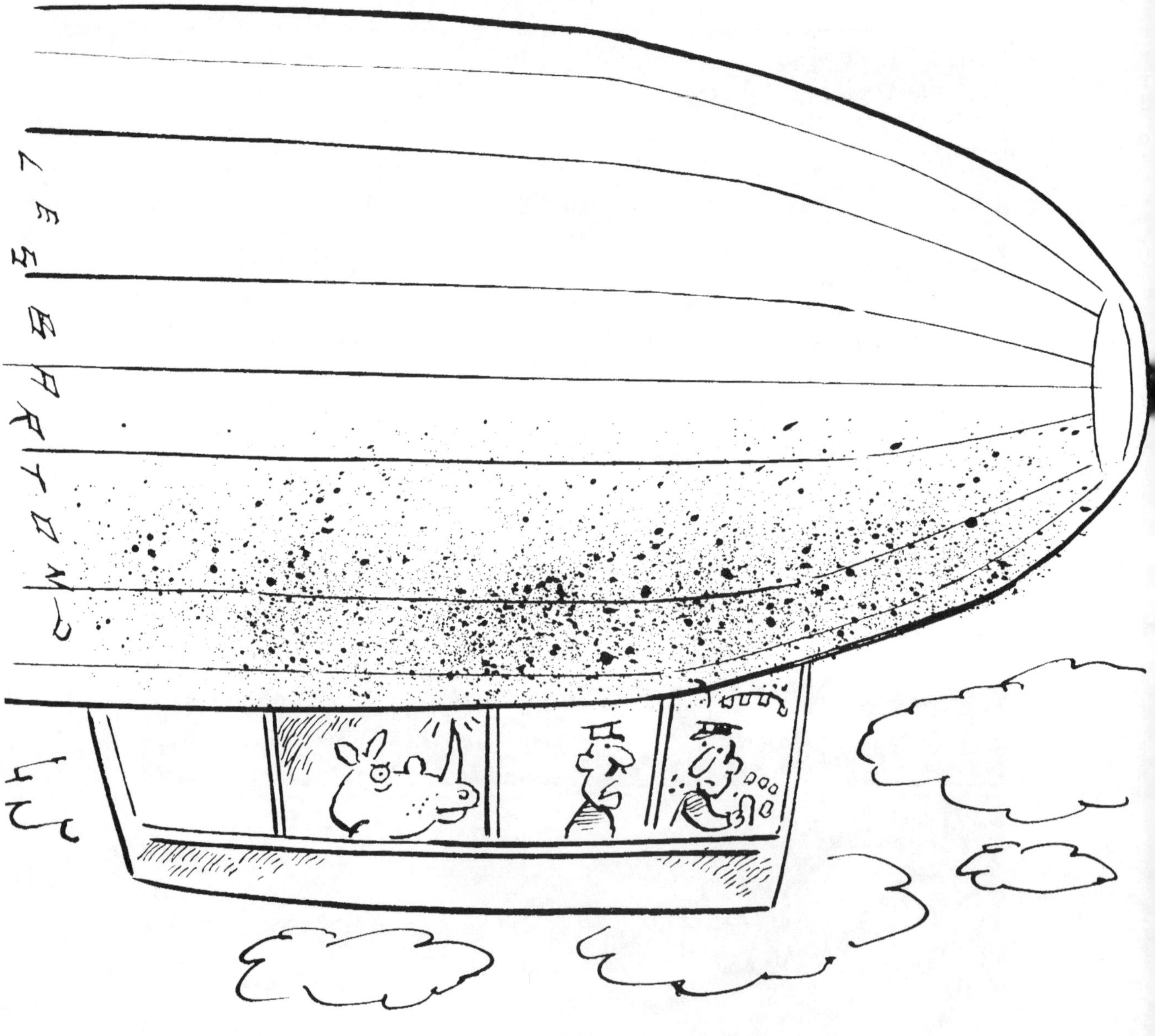

'We have a terrorist on board, sir'

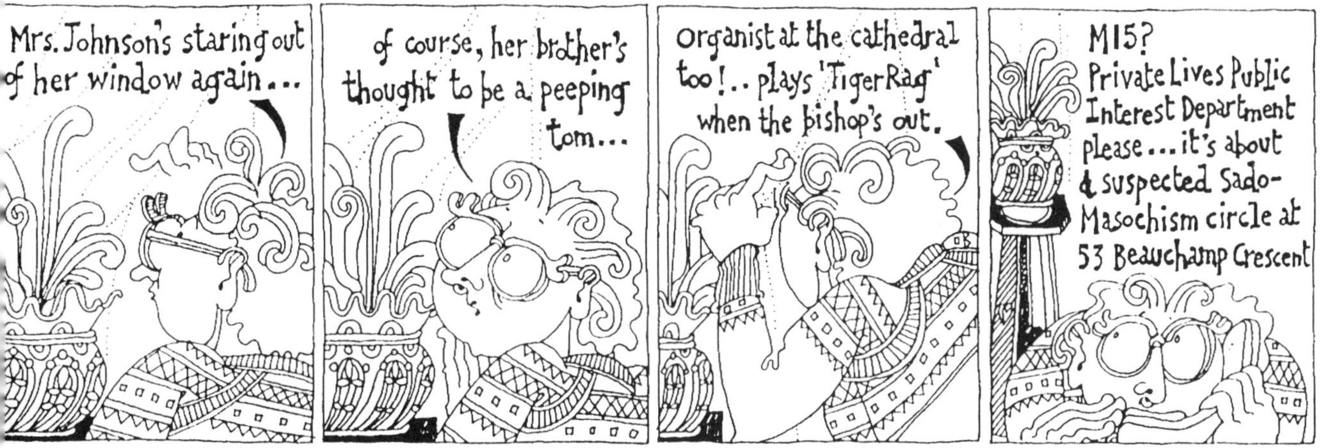
Mrs. Johnson's staring out of her window again...
of course, her brother's thought to be a peeping tom...
Organist at the cathedral too!.. plays 'Tiger Rag' when the bishop's out.
M15?
Private Lives Public Interest Department please... it's about a suspected Sado-Masochism circle at 53 Beauchamp Crescent

HIV

by David Shenton

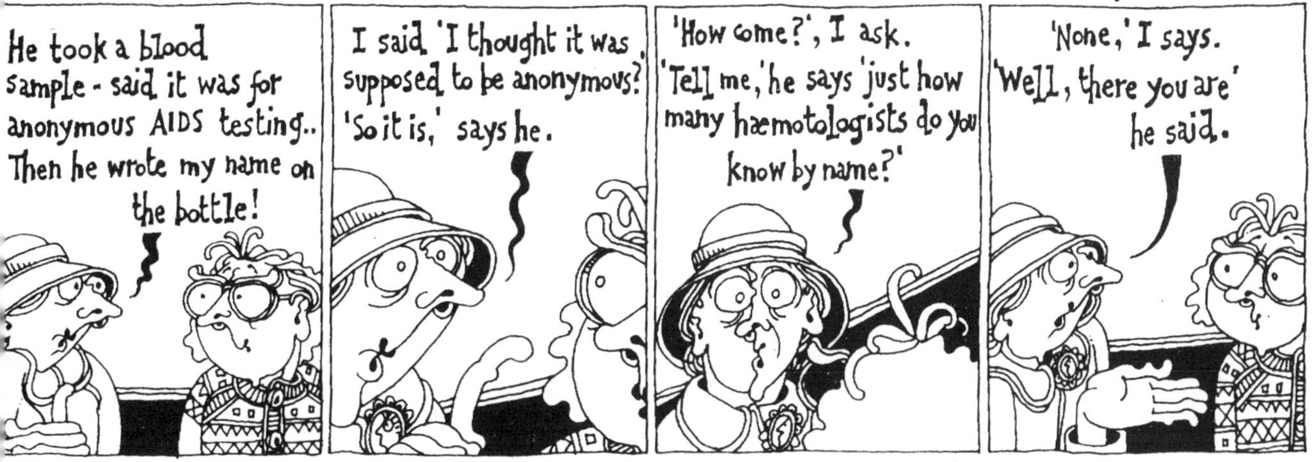
He took a blood sample - said it was for anonymous AIDS testing.. Then he wrote my name on the bottle!
I said 'I thought it was supposed to be anonymous?' 'So it is,' says he.
'How come?', I ask. 'Tell me,' he says 'just how many hæmotologists do you know by name?'
'None,' I says. 'Well, there you are' he said.

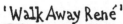

'Walk Away René'

by David Shenton

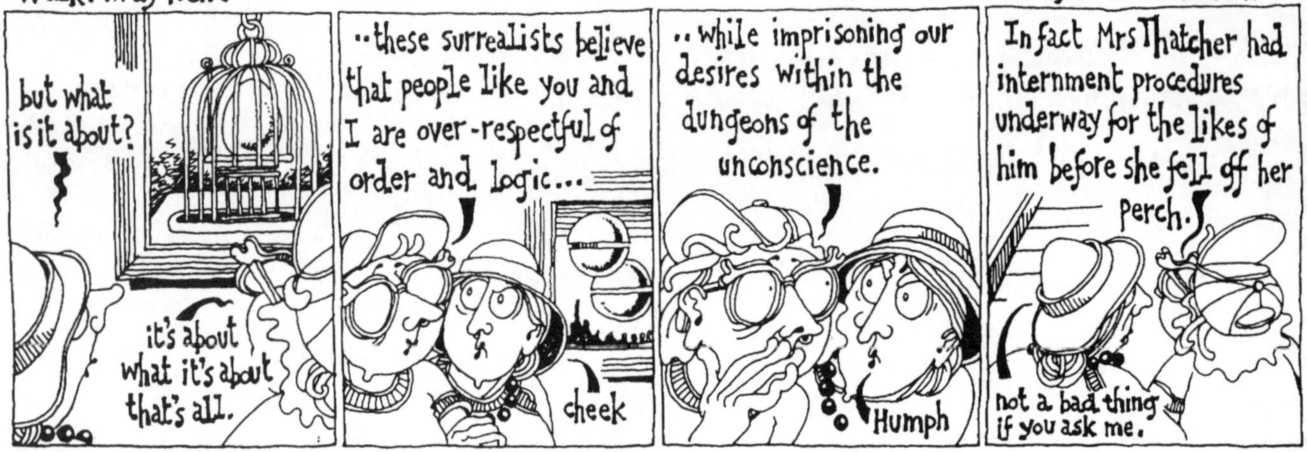
but what is it about?
it's about what it's about that's all.
..these surrealists believe that people like you and I are over-respectful of order and logic...
cheek
..while imprisoning our desires within the dungeons of the unconscience.
Humph
In fact Mrs Thatcher had internment procedures underway for the likes of him before she fell off her perch.
not a bad thing if you ask me.

'The Bitch is Back'

by David Shenton

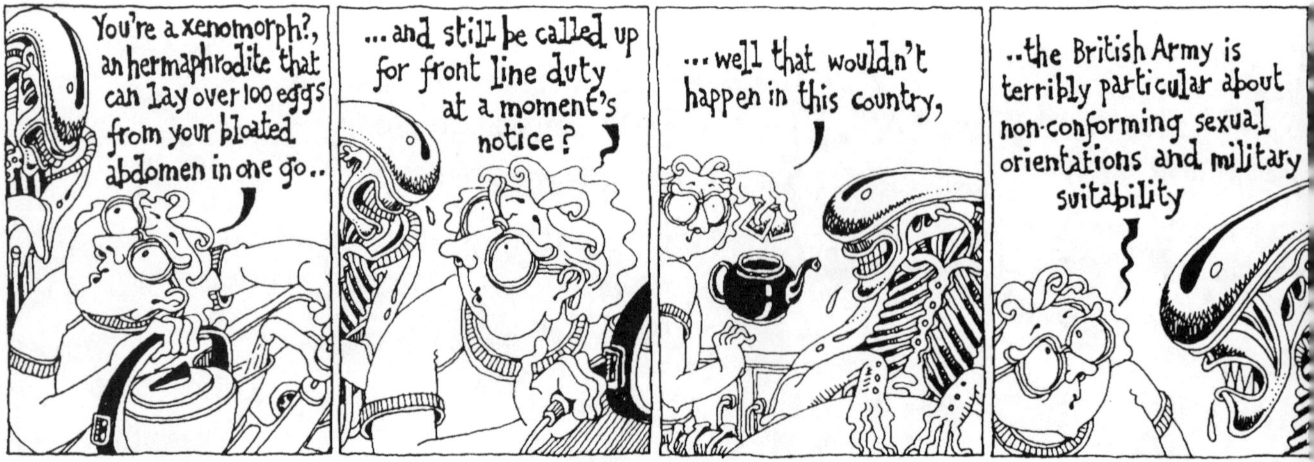
You're a xenomorph?, an hermaphrodite that can lay over 100 eggs from your bloated abdomen in one go..
...and still be called up for front line duty at a moment's notice?
...well that wouldn't happen in this country,
..the British Army is terribly particular about non-conforming sexual orientations and military suitability

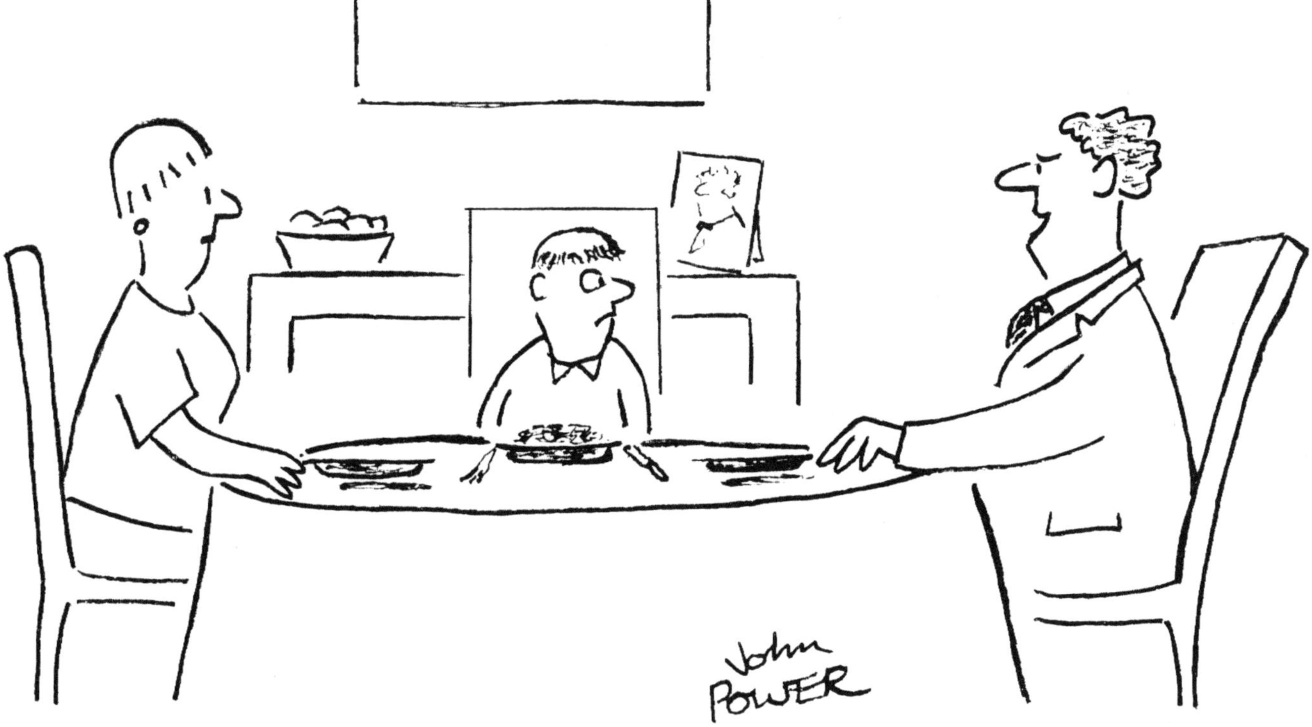
John
POWER

'You can phone Amnesty International <u>AFTER</u> you've eaten your greens'

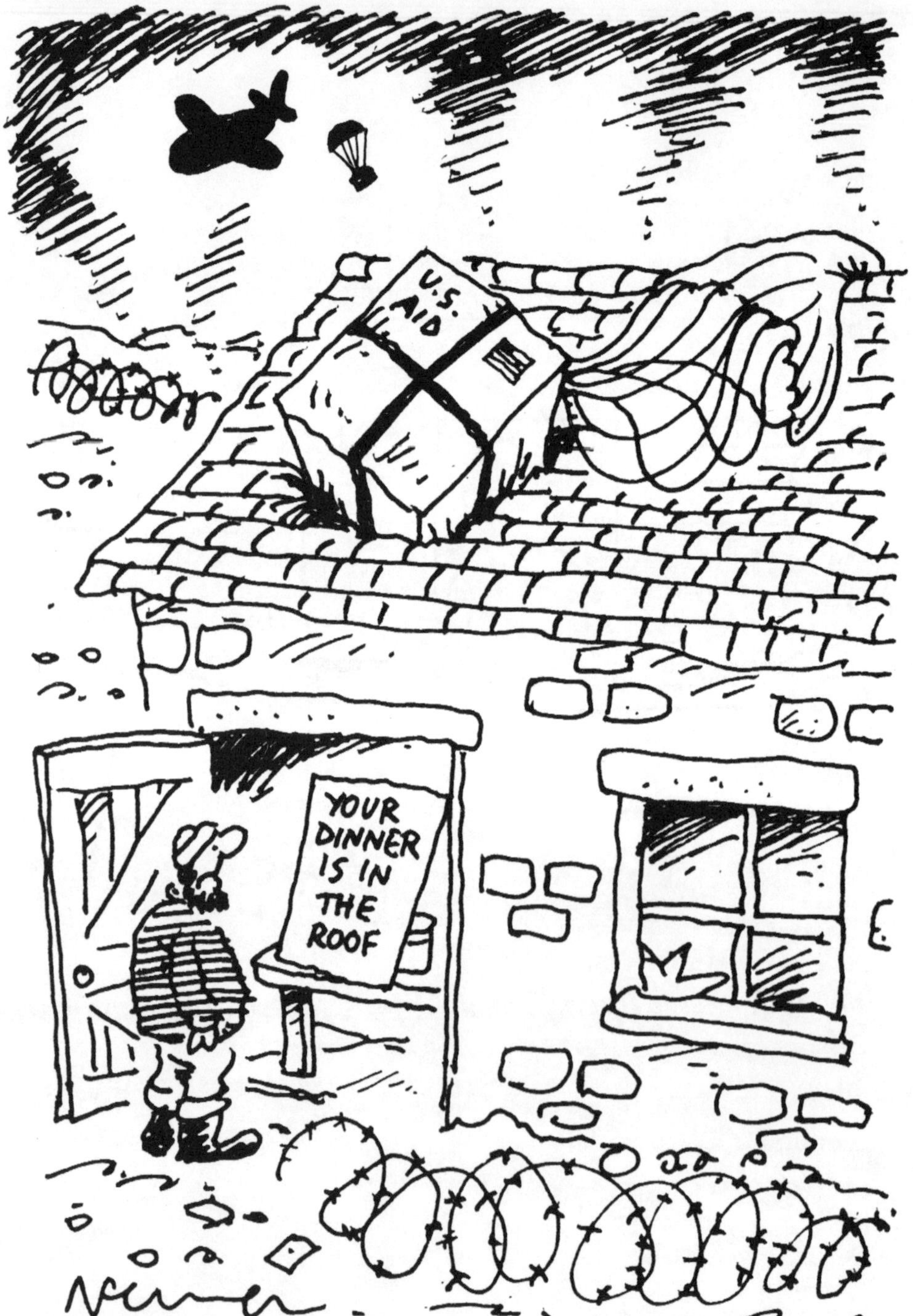
U.S. AID
YOUR DINNER IS IN THE ROOF

'Anything I say will be taken down
and used in evidence against you'

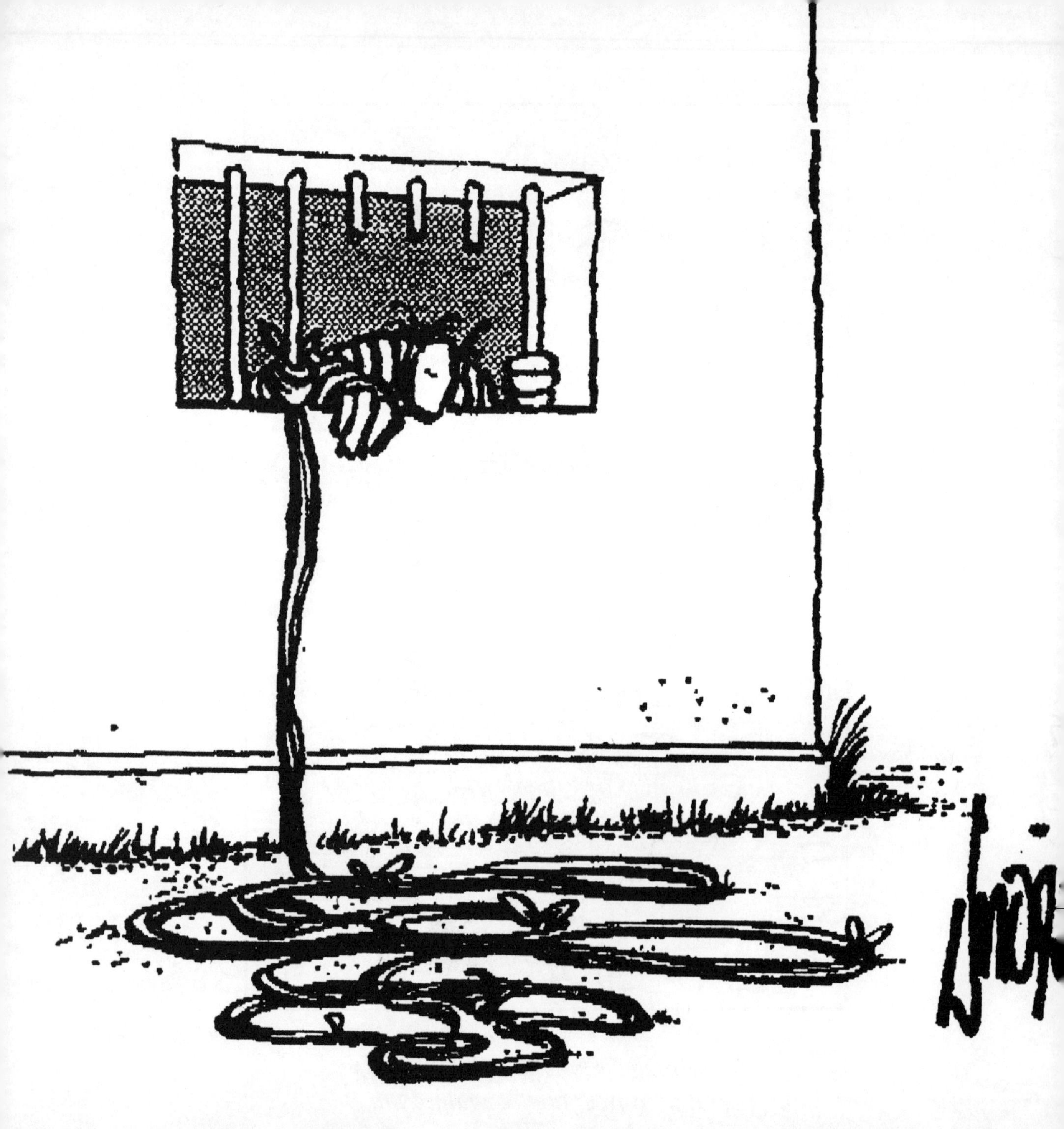

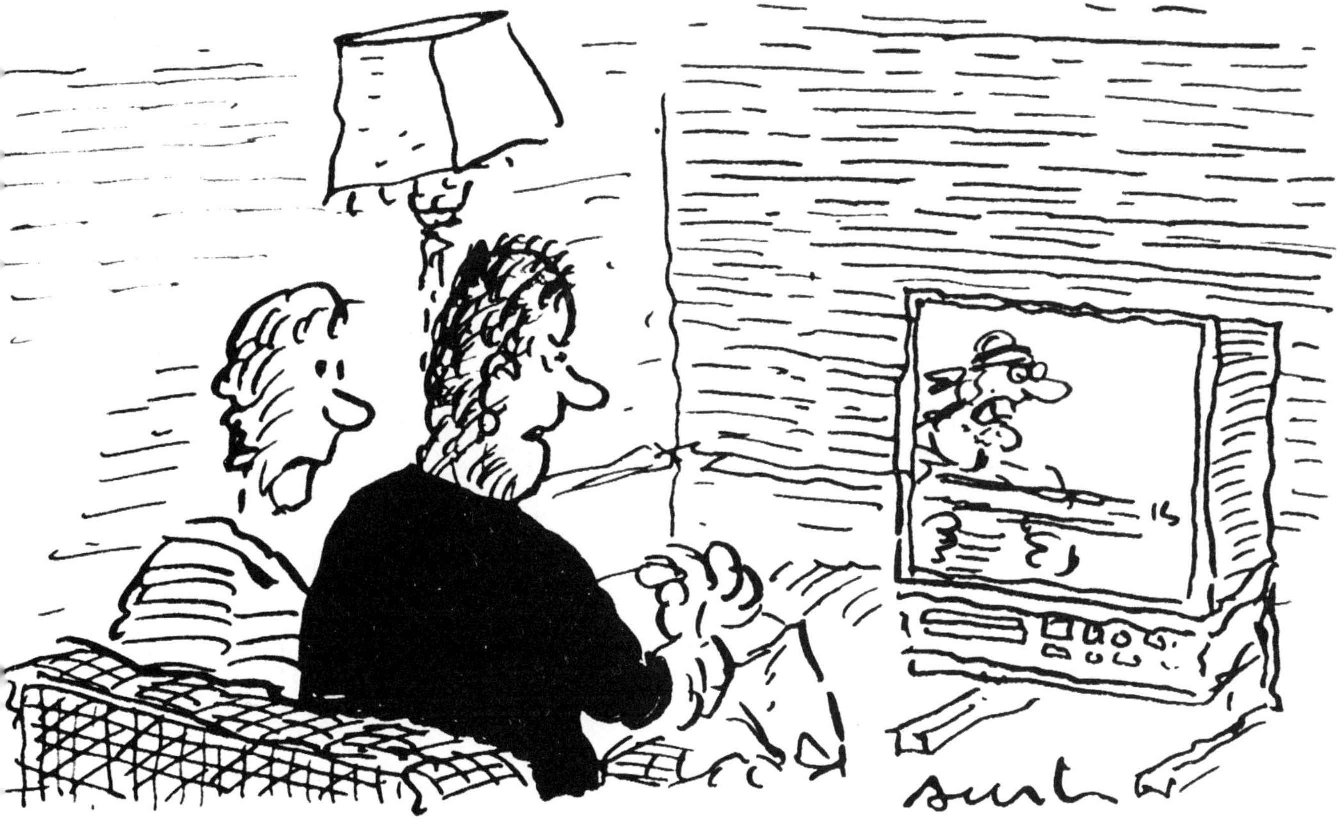

'It is NOT gratuitous violence. This video cost me a tenner'

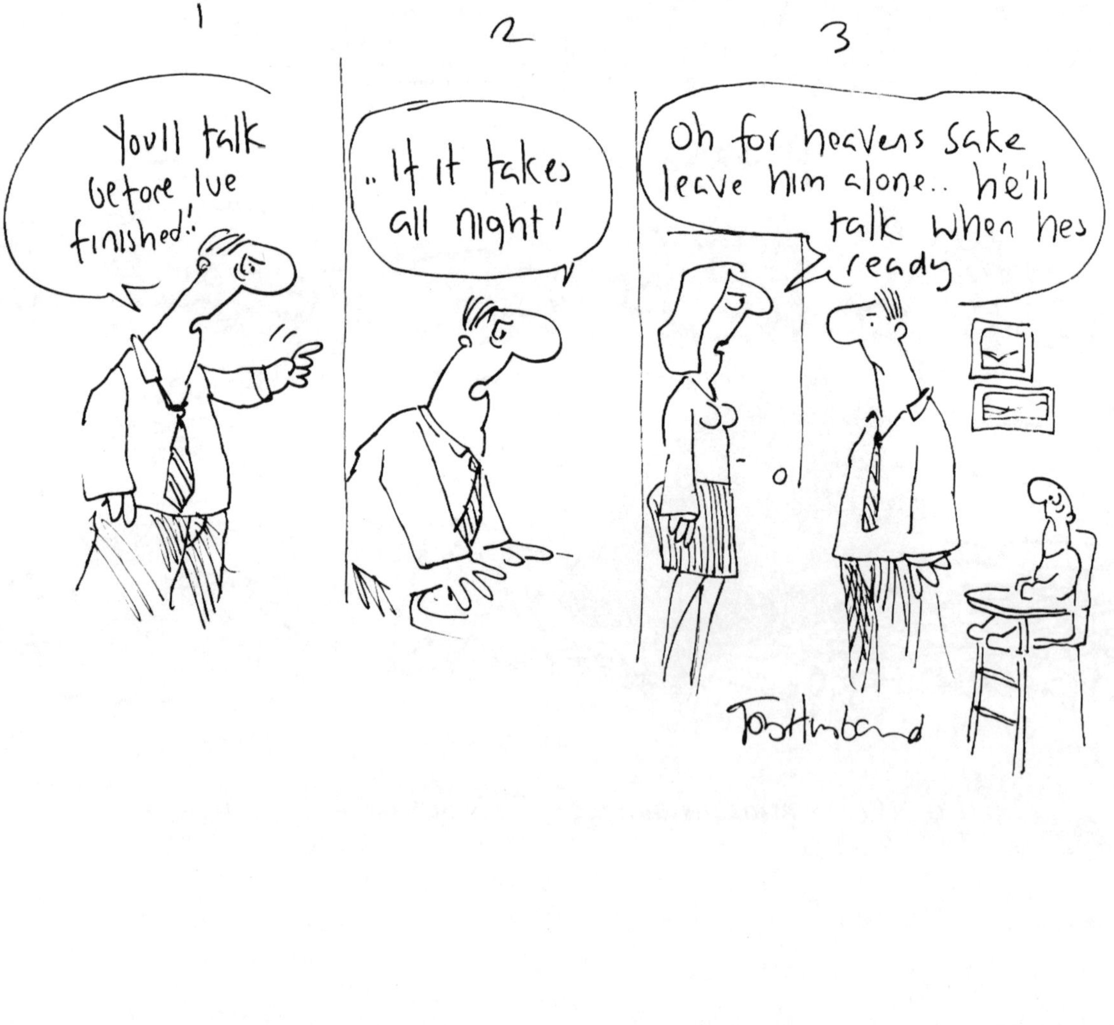
1
2
3
Youll talk before Ive finished!
.. If it takes all night!
Oh for heavens sake leave him alone.. he'll talk when hes ready
Tony Husband

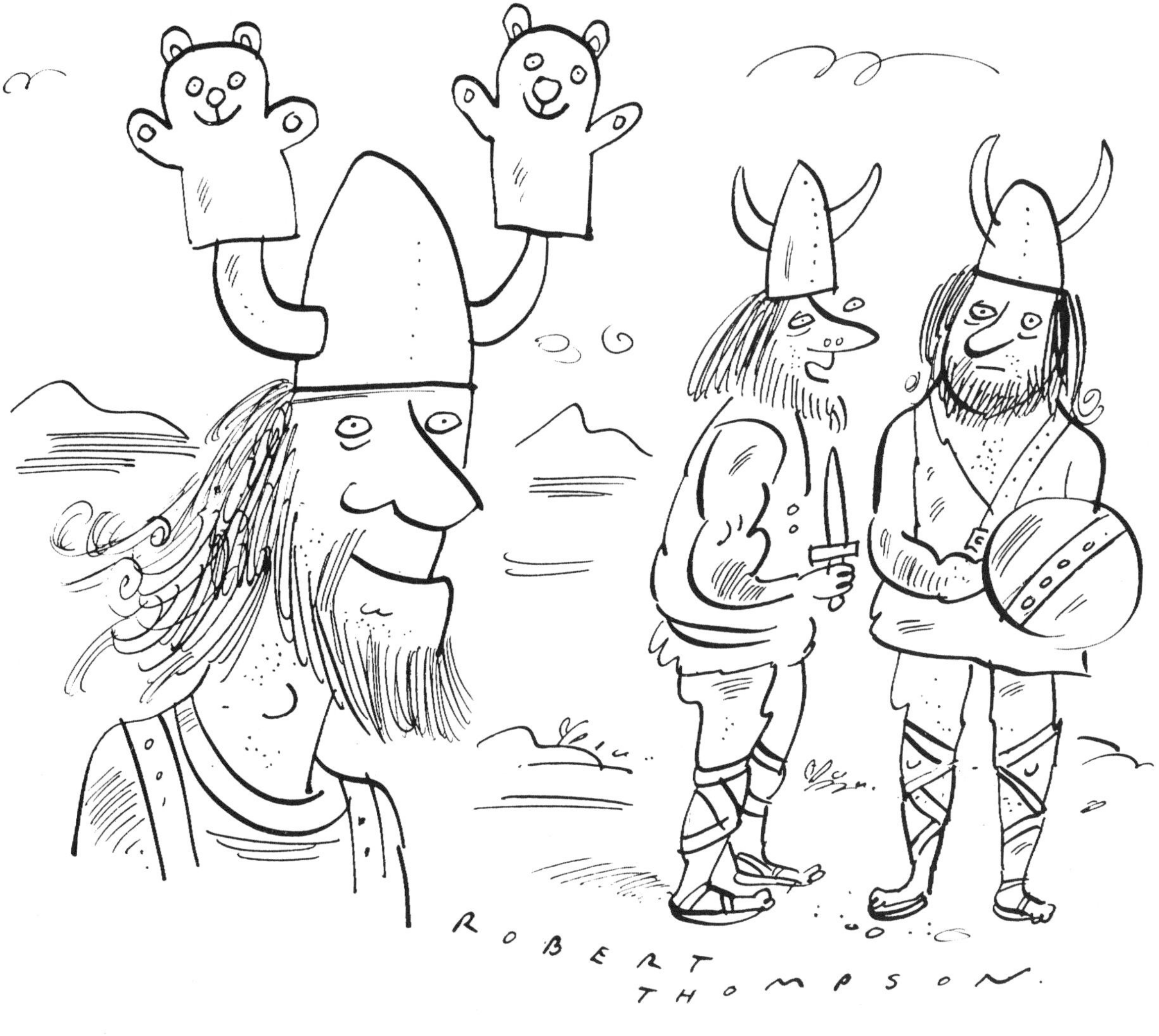
ROBERT THOMPSON.

'Apparently he's great with kids'

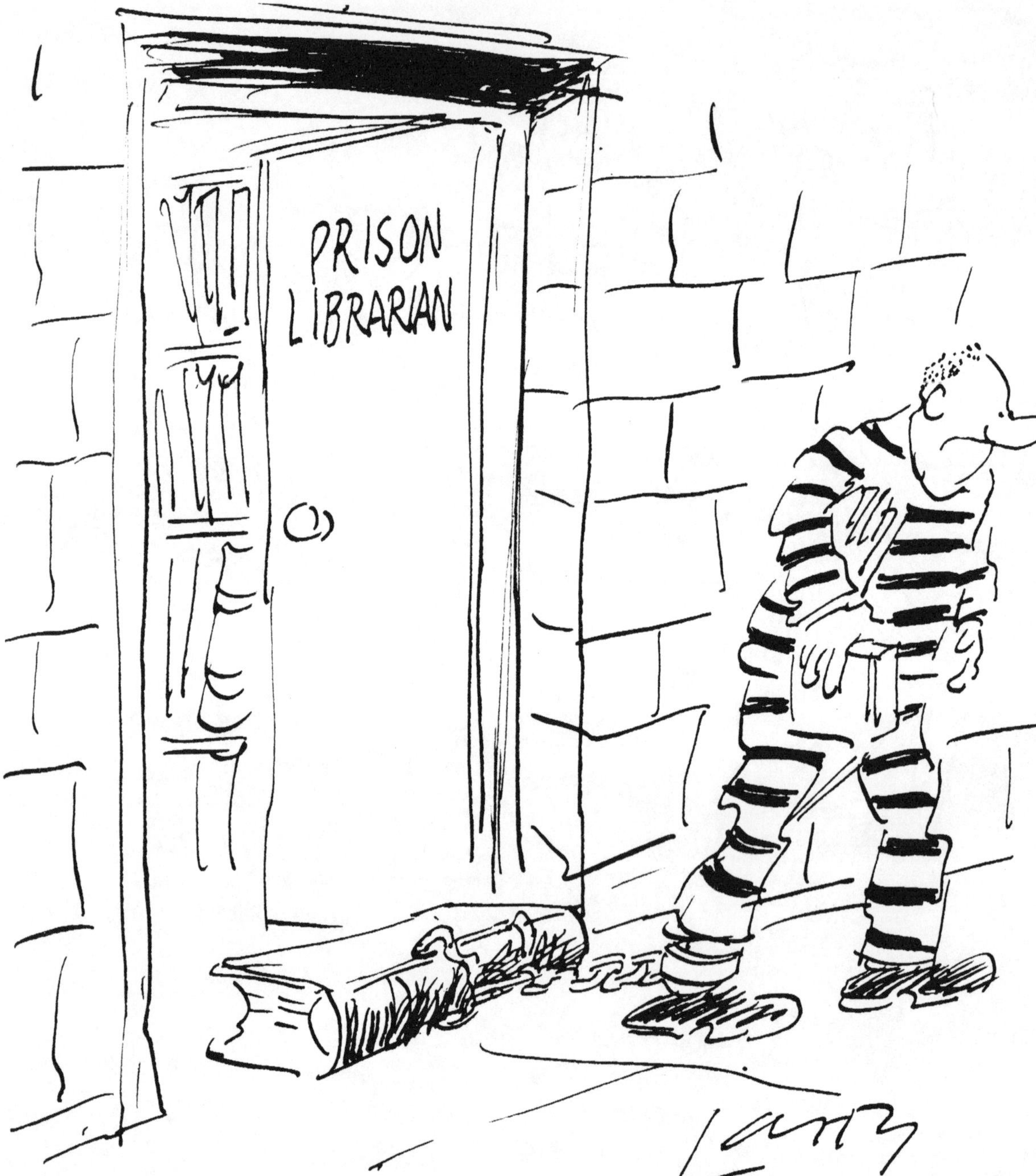
PRISON
LIBRARIAN
Larry

Worthless pursuits No. 51. Trying to impress the neighbours with your hunting trophies

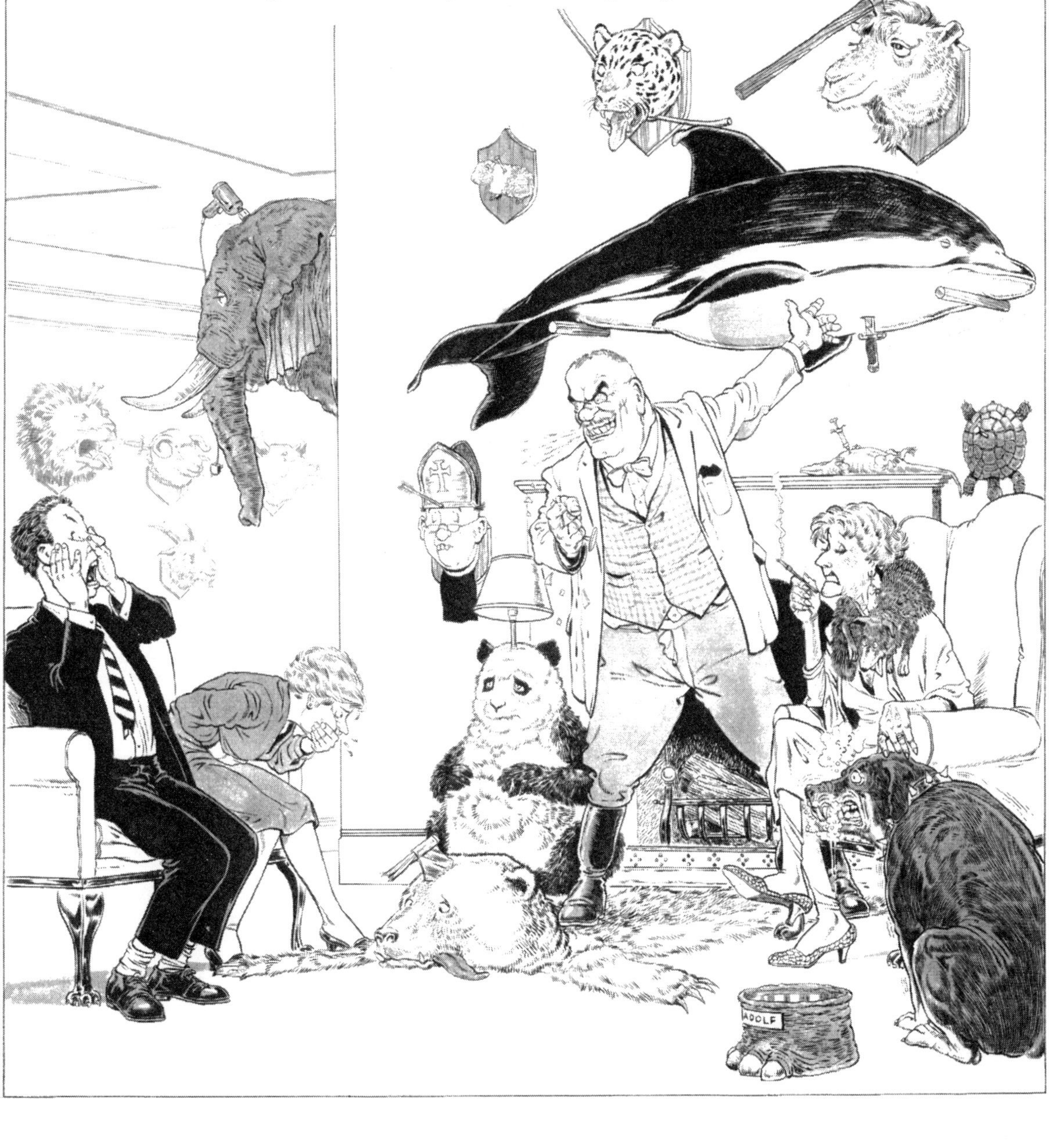
ADOLF

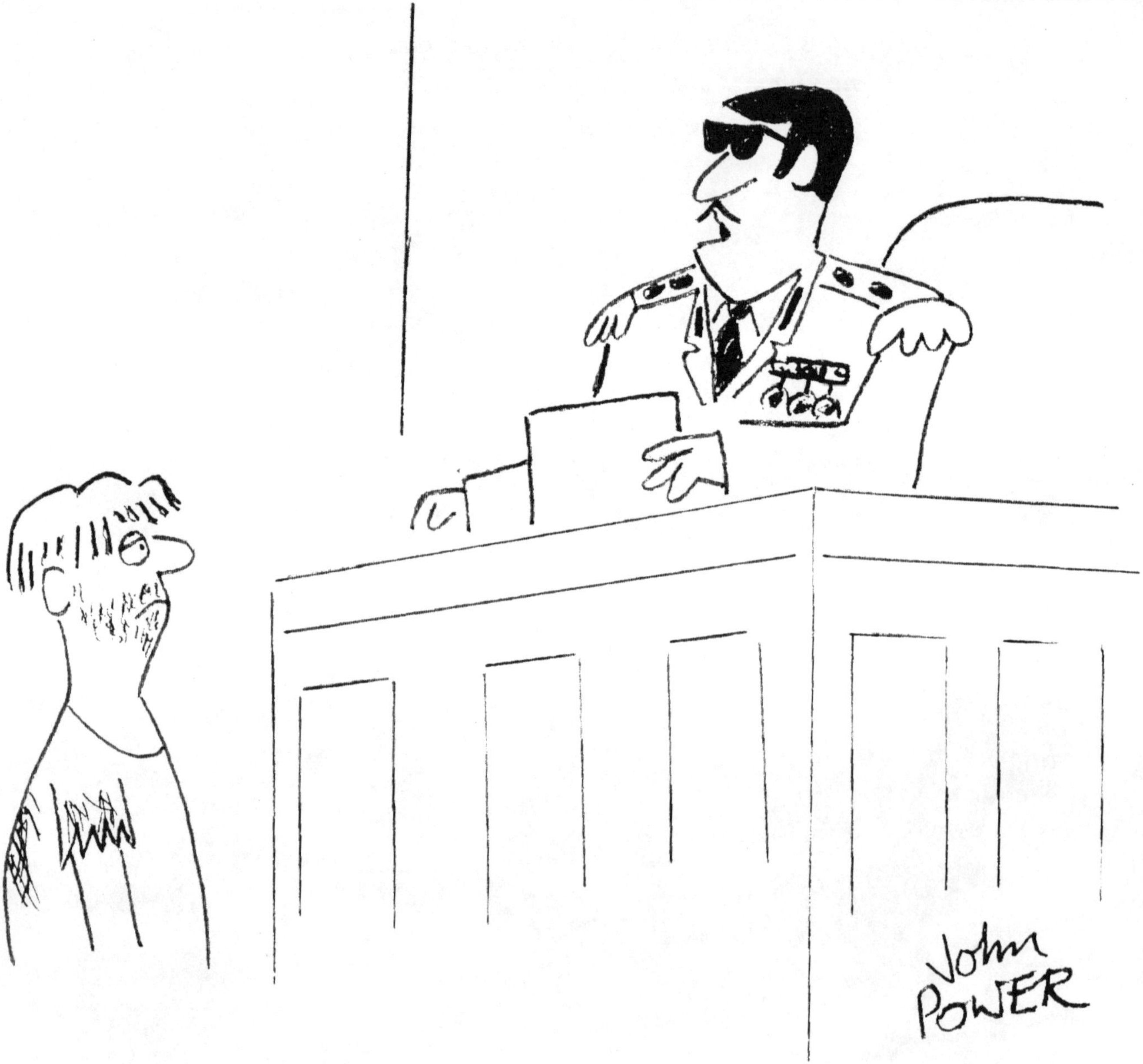
John POWER

'The military court finds you guilty on all trumped up charges'

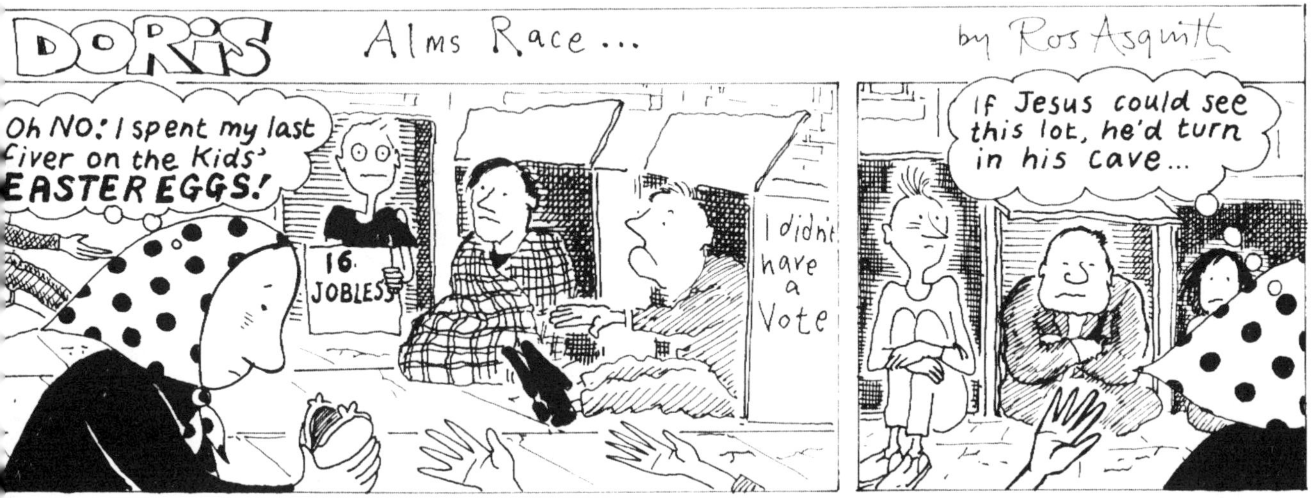
DORIS
Alms Race ...
by Ros Asquith
Oh NO! I spent my last fiver on the Kids' EASTER EGGS!
16 JOBLESS
I didn't have a Vote
If Jesus could see this lot, he'd turn in his cave...

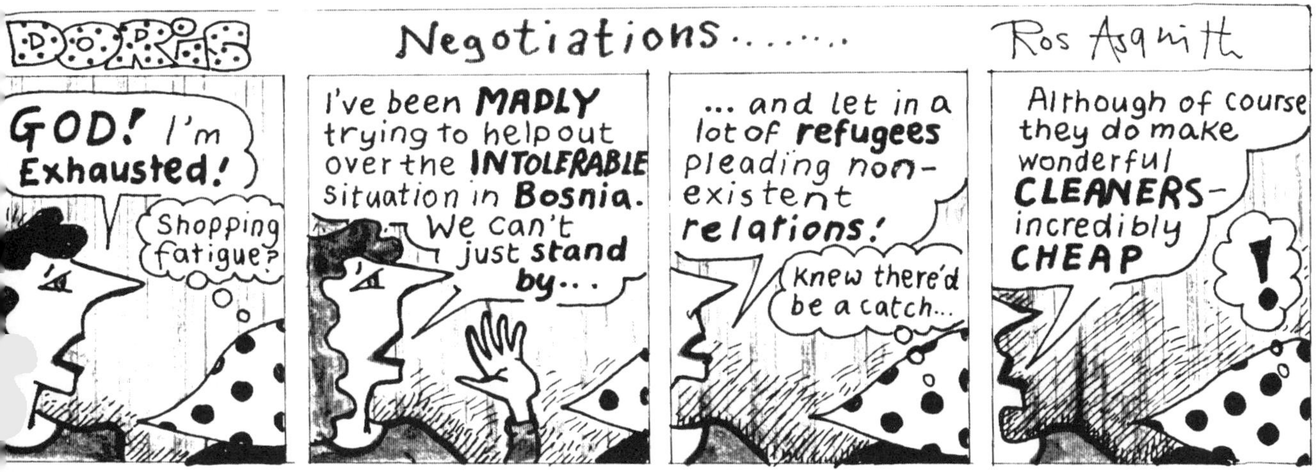
DORIS
Negotiations.......
Ros Asquith
GOD! I'm Exhausted!
Shopping fatigue?
I've been MADLY trying to help out over the INTOLERABLE situation in Bosnia.
We can't just stand by...
... and let in a lot of refugees pleading non-existent relations!
Knew there'd be a catch...
Although of course they do make wonderful CLEANERS - incredibly CHEAP
!

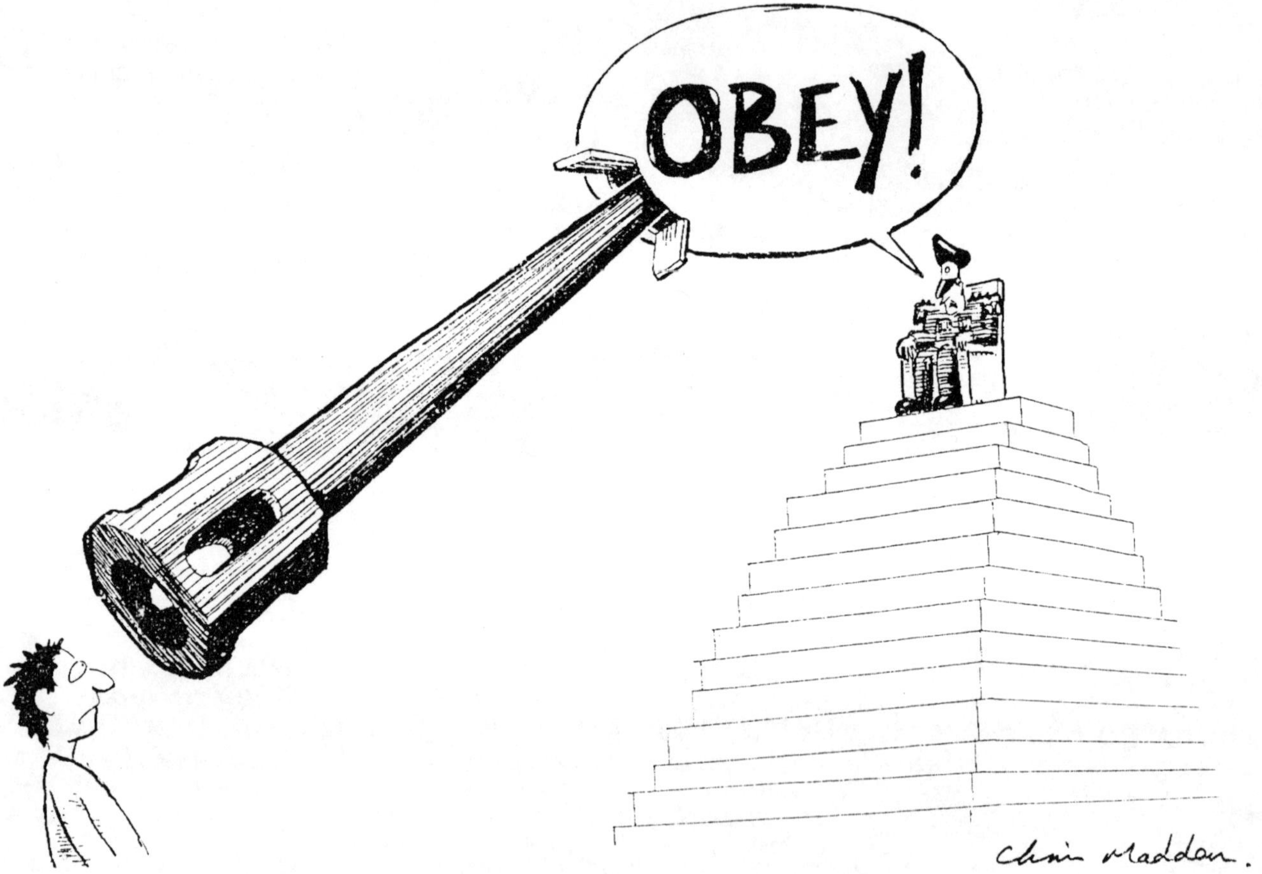
OBEY!
Chris Madden.

The Military Dictator

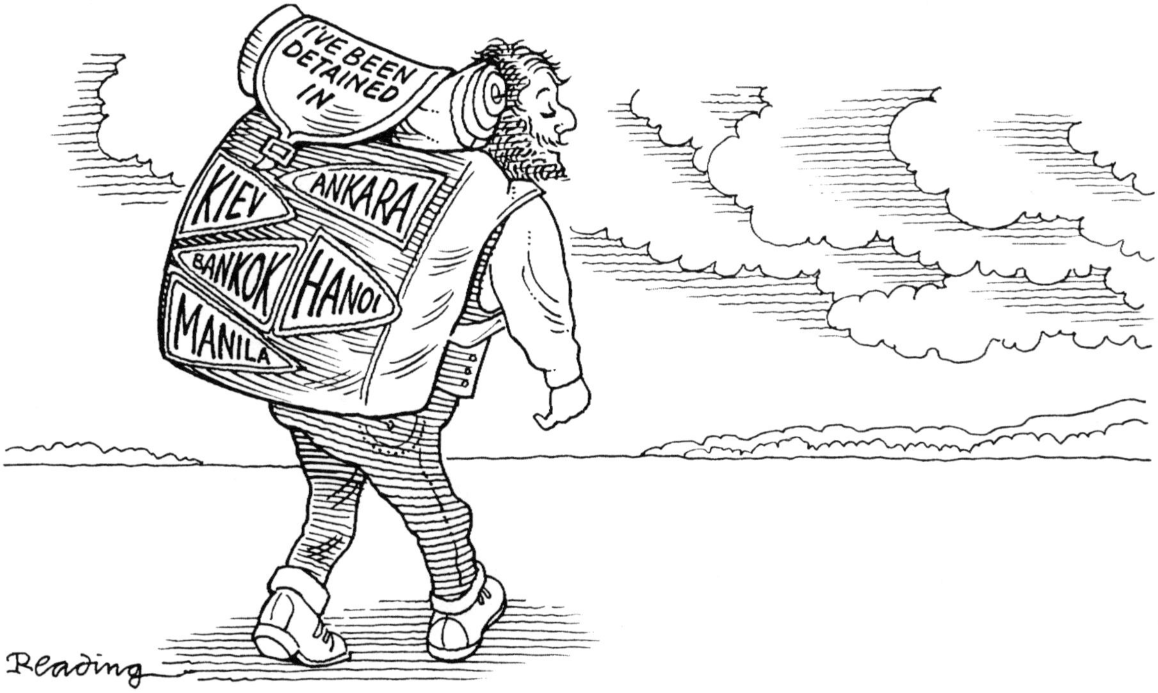
I'VE BEEN DETAINED IN
KIEV
ANKARA
BANKOK
HANOI
MANILA
Reading

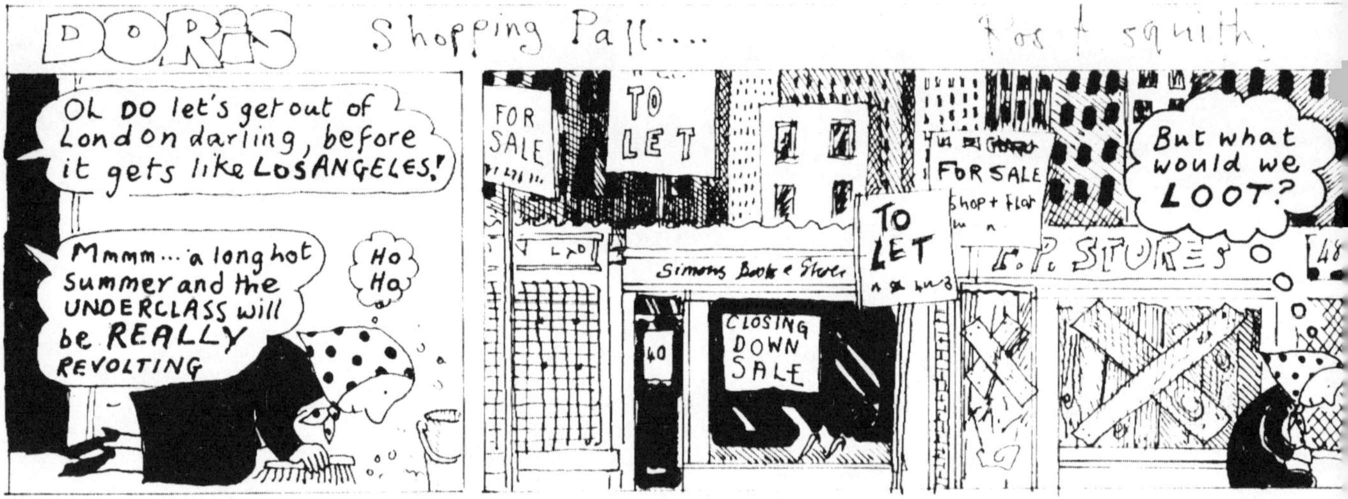

DORIS
Shopping Pall....
Ros Asquith
Oh DO let's get out of London darling, before it gets like LOS ANGELES!
Mmmm... a long hot summer and the UNDERCLASS will be REALLY REVOLTING
Ho Ha
FOR SALE
TO LET
FOR SALE
Shop + Flat
TO LET
Simons Books & Stores
CLOSING DOWN SALE
40
STORES
But what would we LOOT?

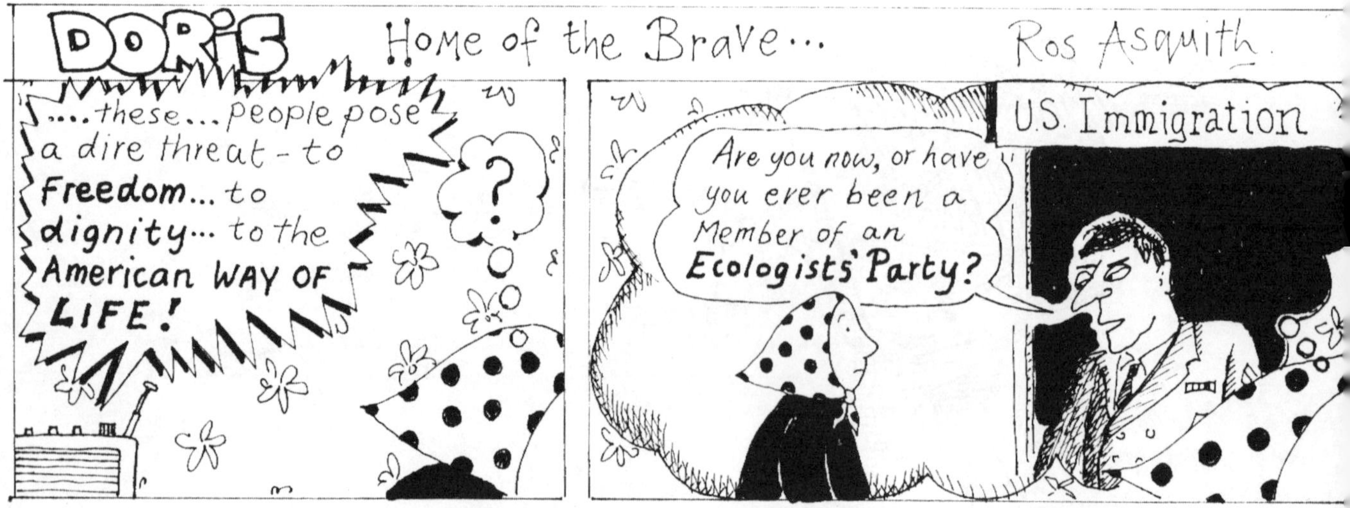

DORIS
Home of the Brave...
Ros Asquith
....these...people pose a dire threat - to Freedom... to dignity... to the American WAY OF LIFE!
?
U.S. Immigration
Are you now, or have you ever been a Member of an Ecologists' Party?

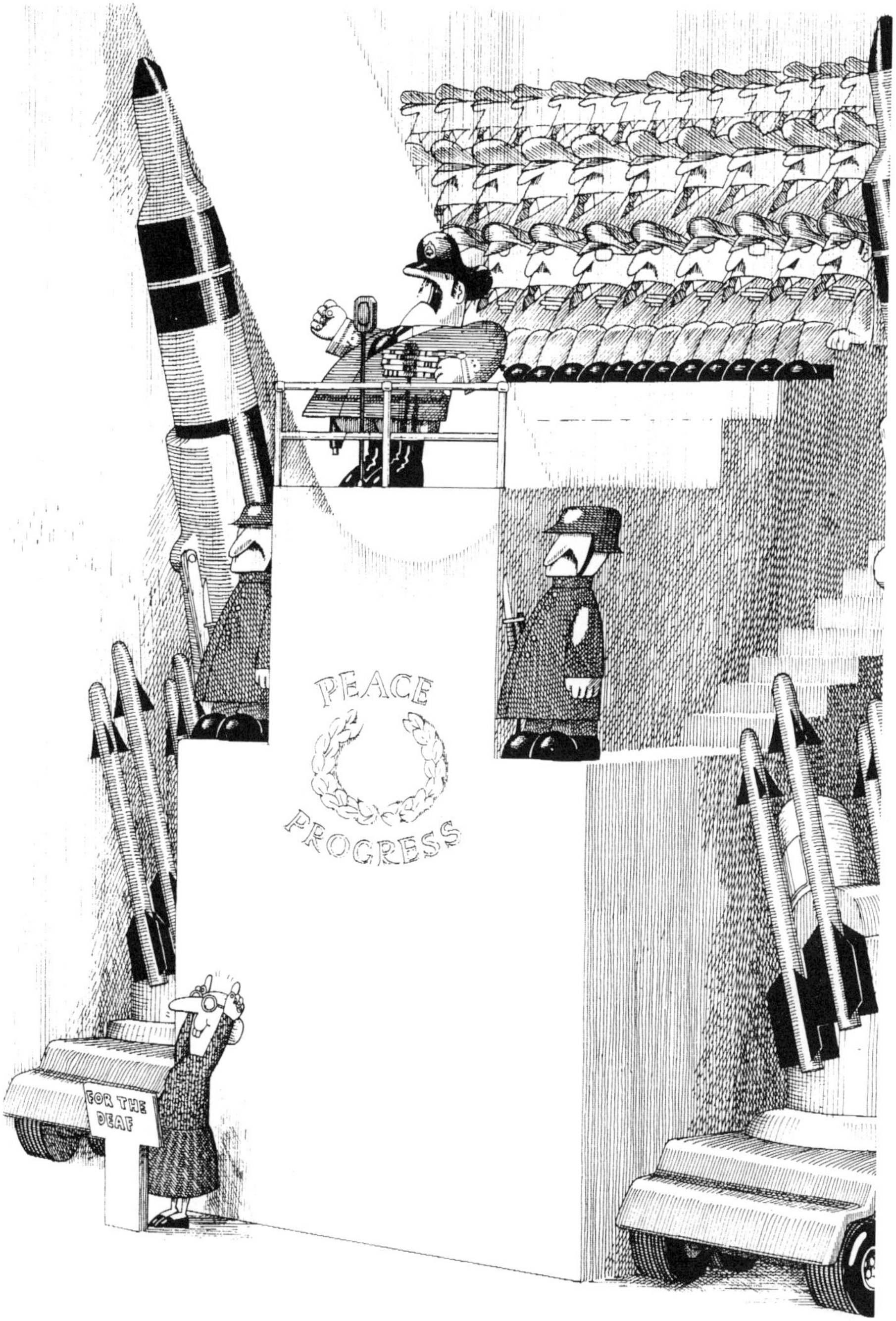
PEACE
PROGRESS
FOR THE DEAF

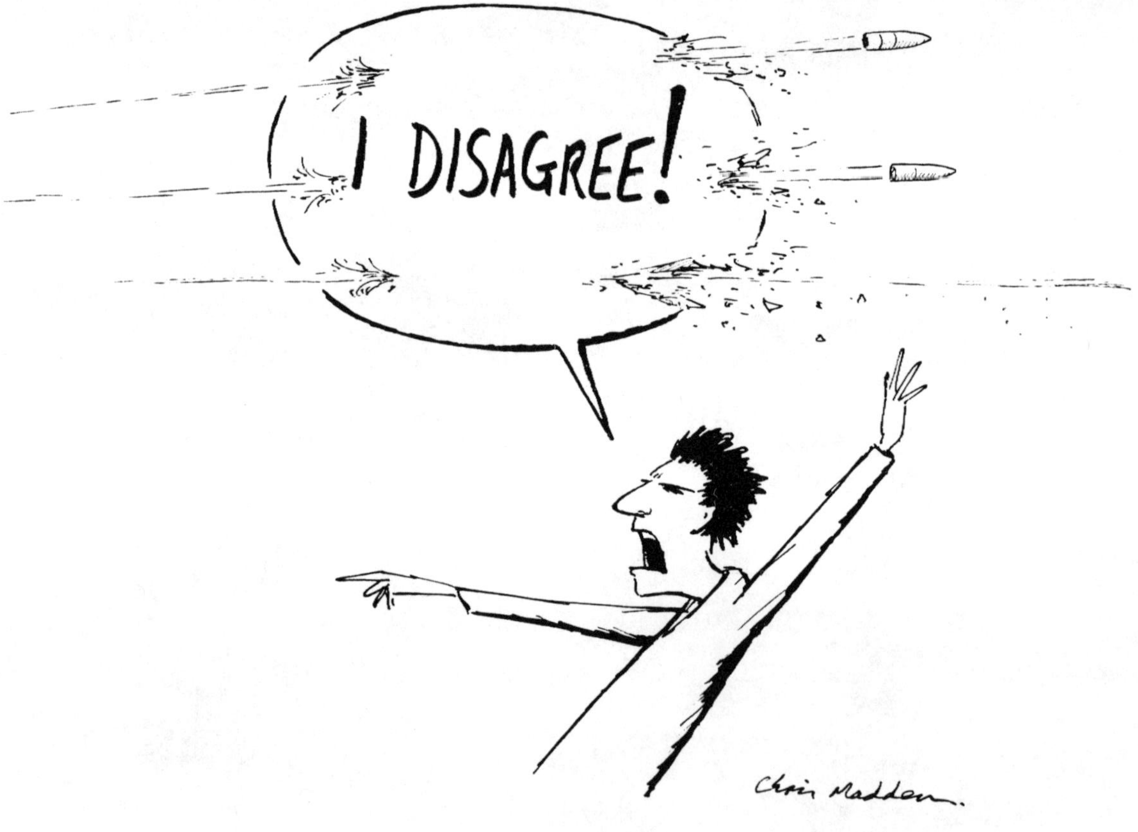
I DISAGREE!
Chris Madden

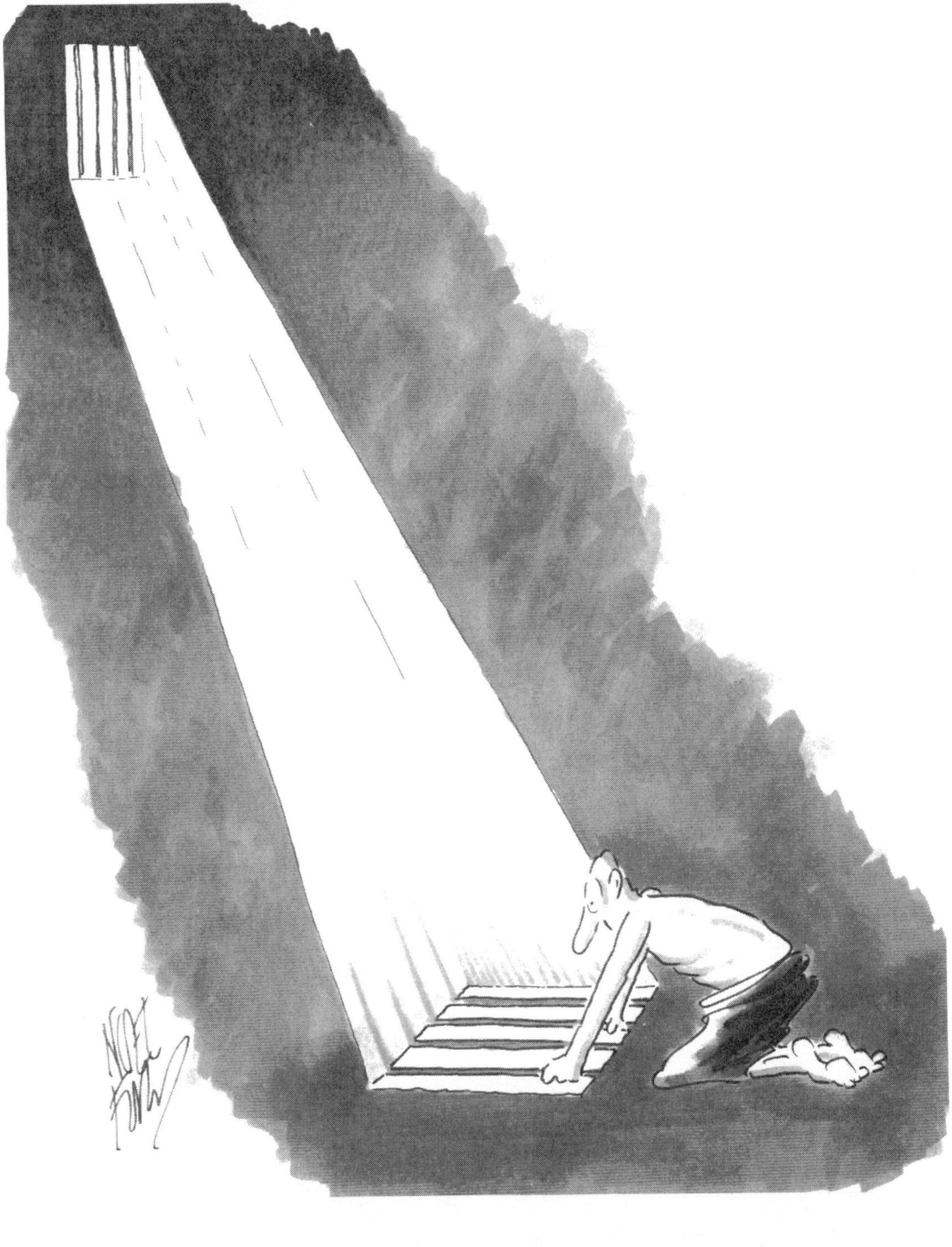

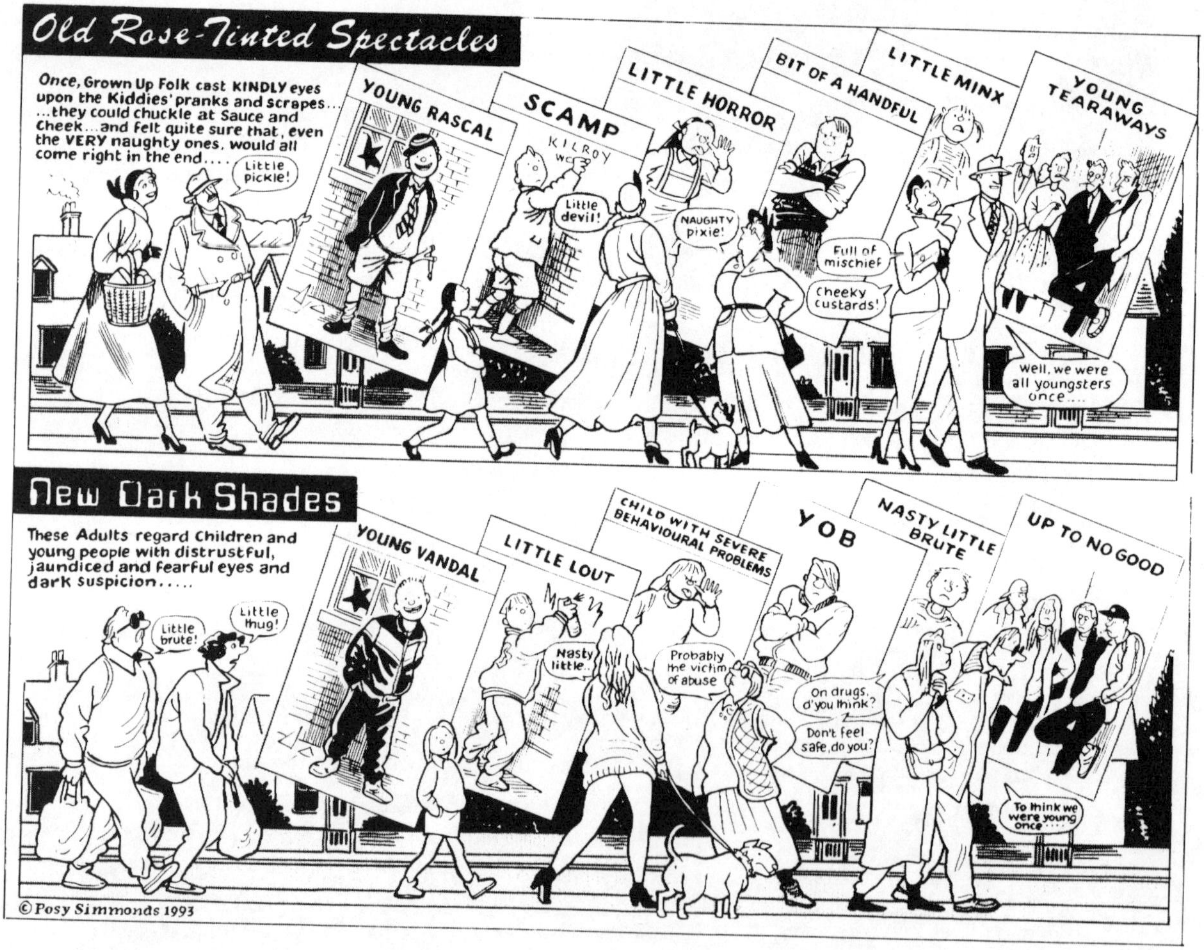
Old Rose-Tinted Spectacles
Once, Grown Up Folk cast KINDLY eyes upon the Kiddies' pranks and scrapes... ...they could chuckle at Sauce and Cheek...and felt quite sure that, even the VERY naughty ones, would all come right in the end....
Little pickle!
YOUNG RASCAL
SCAMP
KILROY WO
Little devil!
LITTLE HORROR
NAUGHTY pixie!
BIT OF A HANDFUL
Full of mischief
Cheeky custards!
LITTLE MINX
YOUNG TEARAWAYS
Well, we were all youngsters once....
New Dark Shades
These Adults regard Children and young people with distrustful, jaundiced and fearful eyes and dark suspicion.....
Little brute!
Little thug!
YOUNG VANDAL
LITTLE LOUT
Nasty little..
CHILD WITH SEVERE BEHAVIOURAL PROBLEMS
Probably the victim of abuse
YOB
On drugs, d'you think?
Don't feel safe, do you?
NASTY LITTLE BRUTE
UP TO NO GOOD
To think we were young once....
© Posy Simmonds 1993

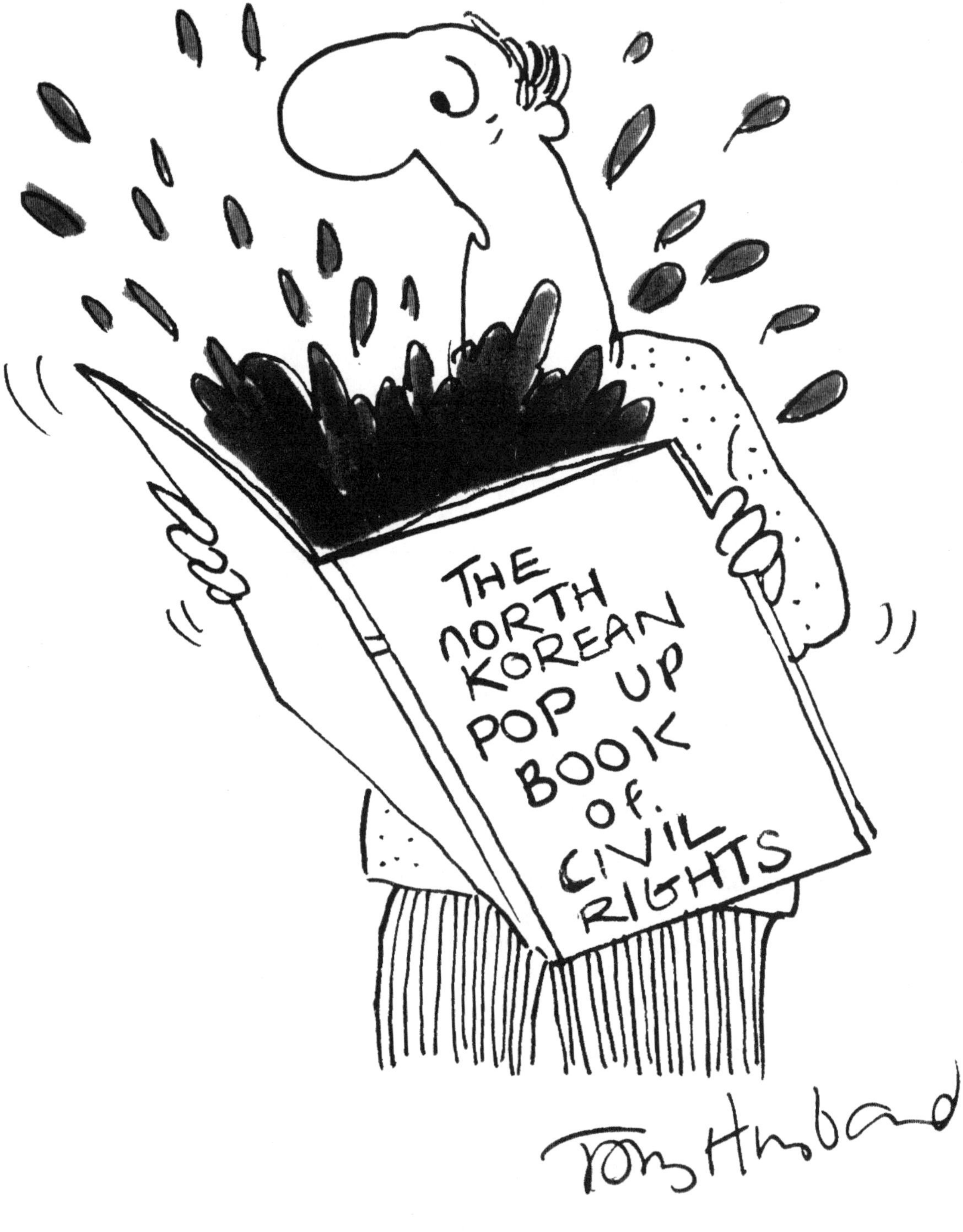
THE NORTH KOREAN POP UP BOOK OF CIVIL RIGHTS
Tom Husband

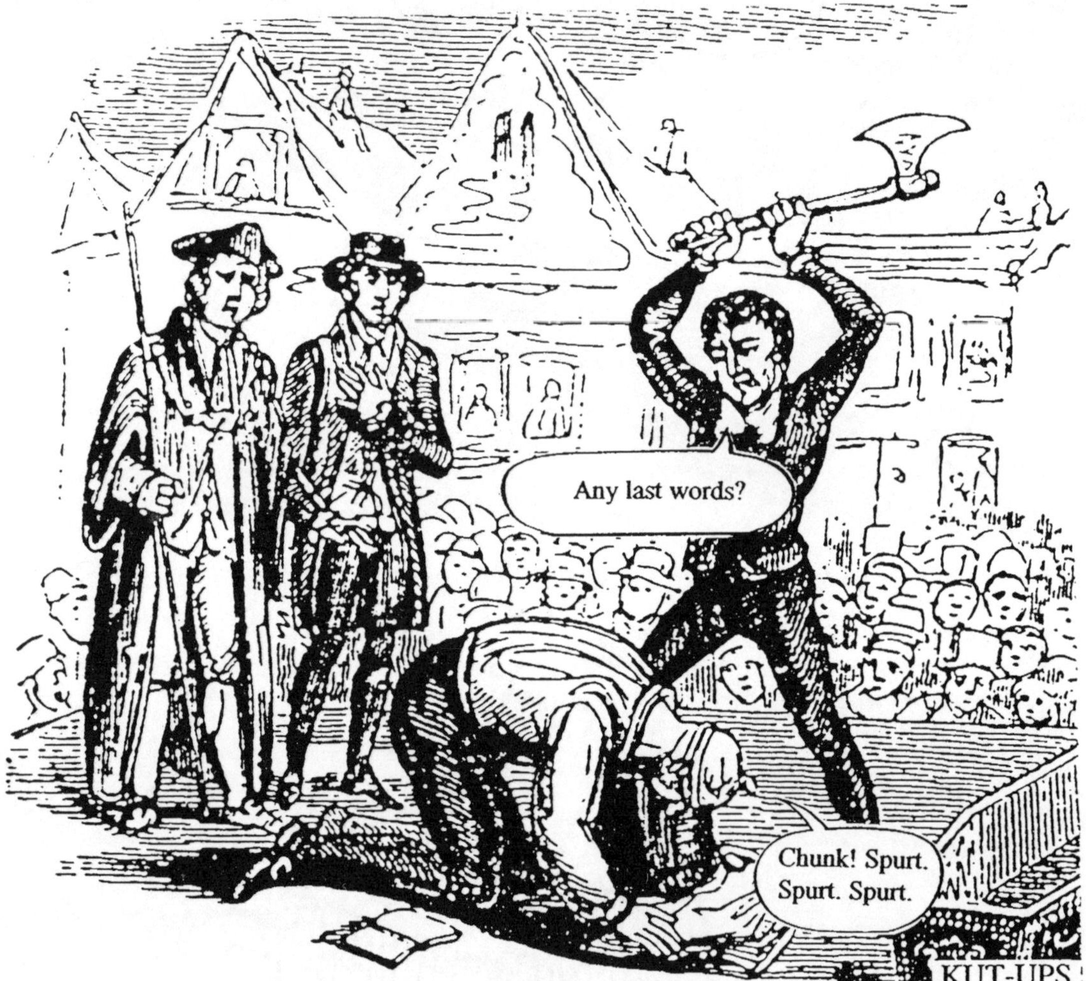
Any last words?
Chunk! Spurt.
Spurt. Spurt.
KUT-UPS

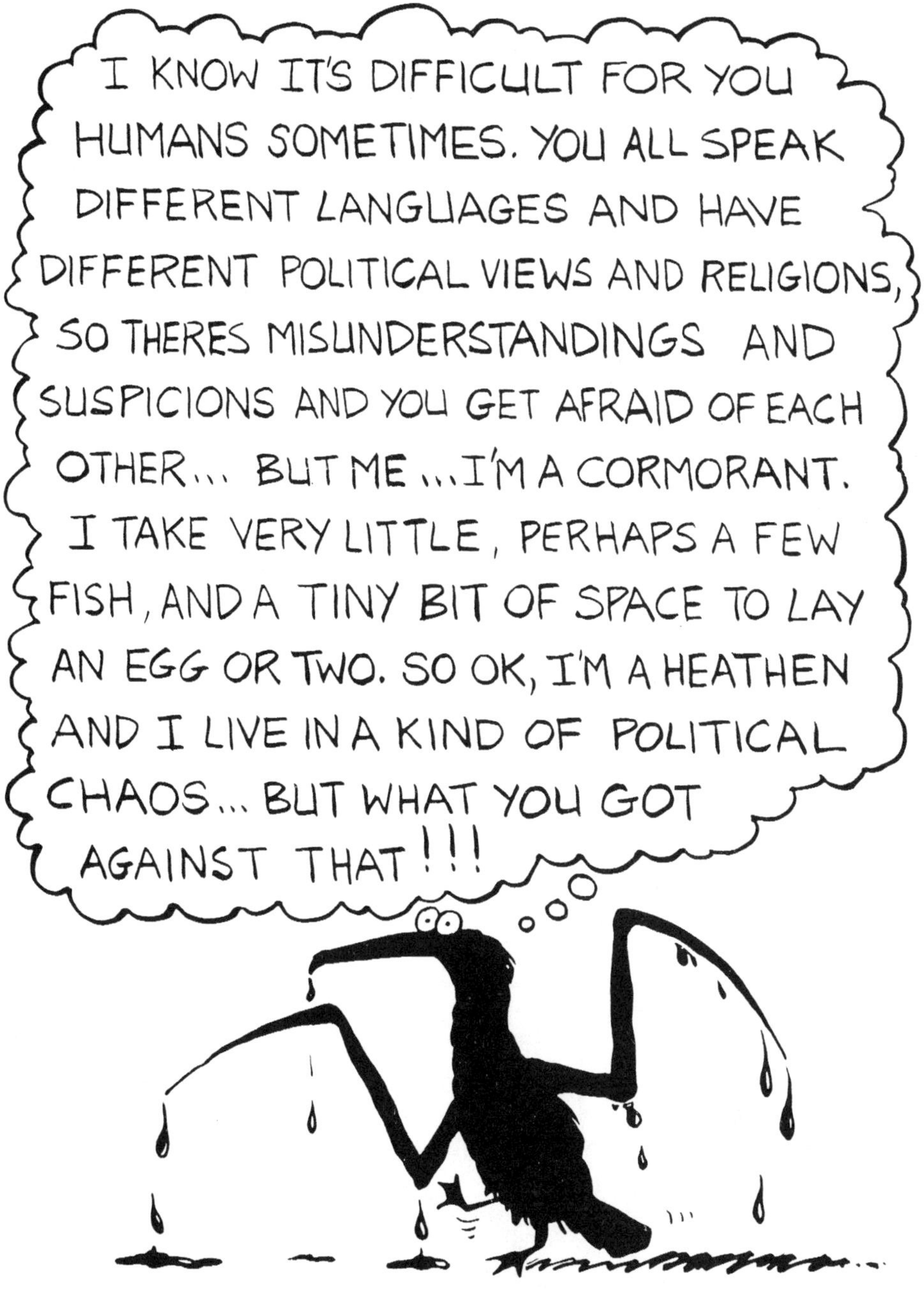
I KNOW IT'S DIFFICULT FOR YOU HUMANS SOMETIMES. YOU ALL SPEAK DIFFERENT LANGUAGES AND HAVE DIFFERENT POLITICAL VIEWS AND RELIGIONS, SO THERES MISUNDERSTANDINGS AND SUSPICIONS AND YOU GET AFRAID OF EACH OTHER... BUT ME ...I'M A CORMORANT. I TAKE VERY LITTLE, PERHAPS A FEW FISH, AND A TINY BIT OF SPACE TO LAY AN EGG OR TWO. SO OK, I'M A HEATHEN AND I LIVE IN A KIND OF POLITICAL CHAOS... BUT WHAT YOU GOT AGAINST THAT!!!

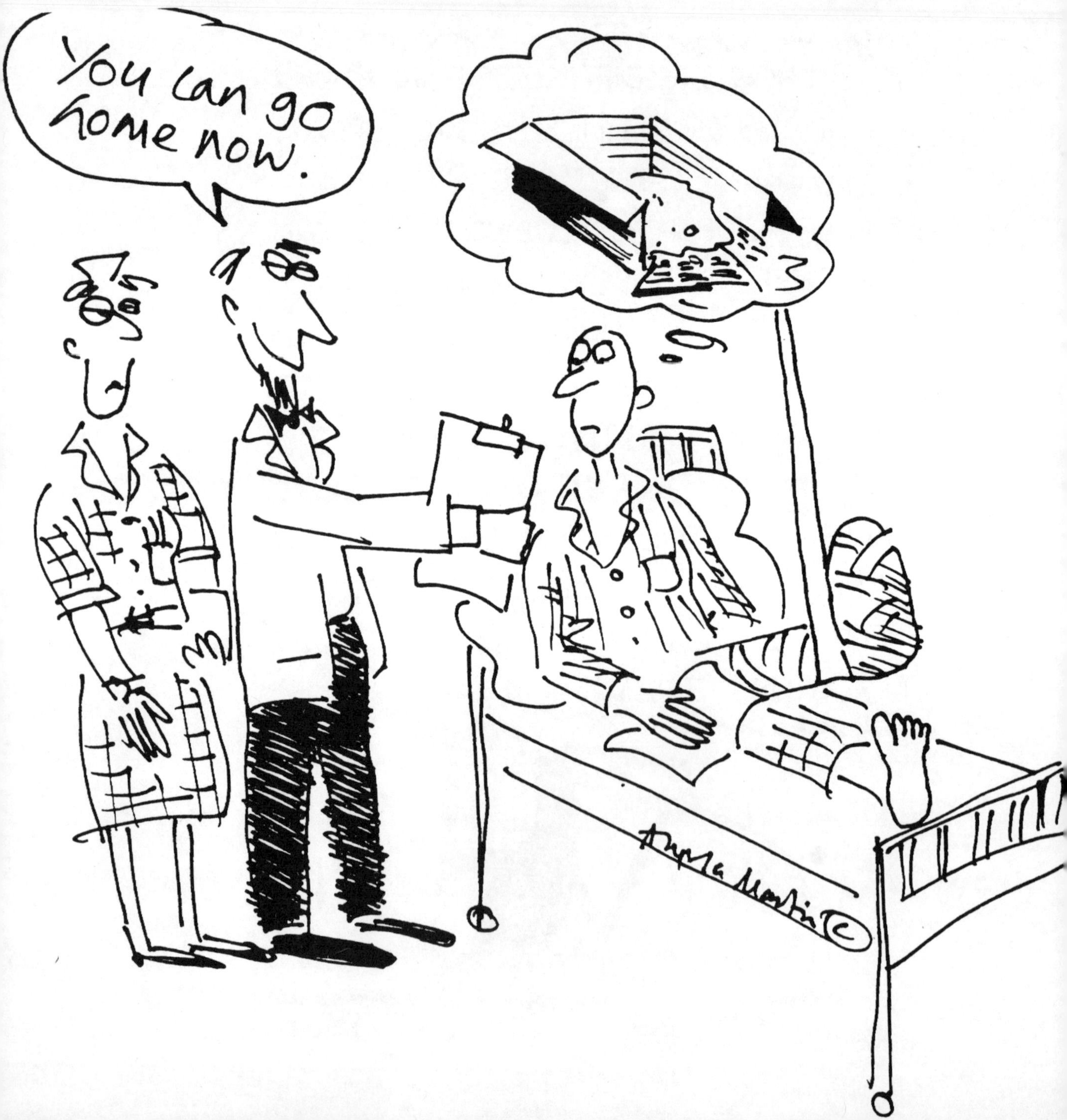
You can go home now.

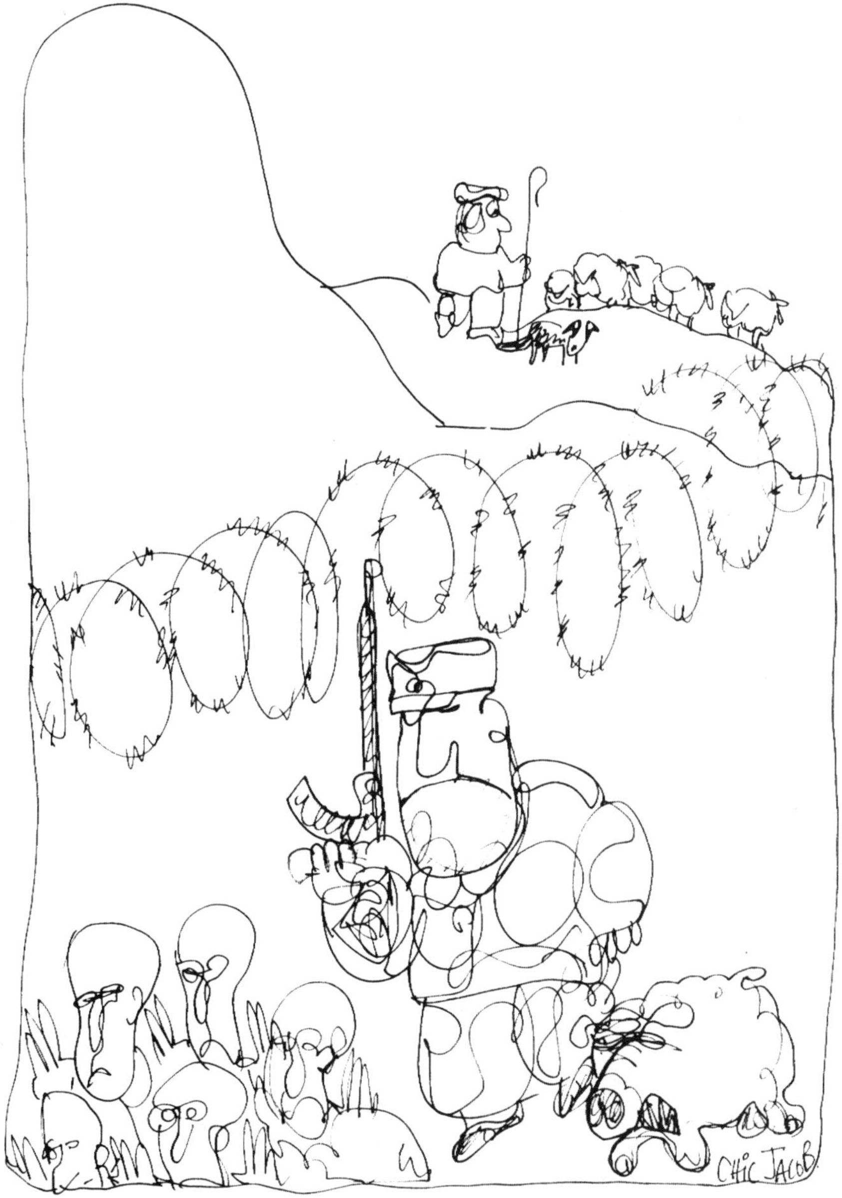
CHIC JACOB

'Hello Amnesty International?
I've been imprisoned without a trial'

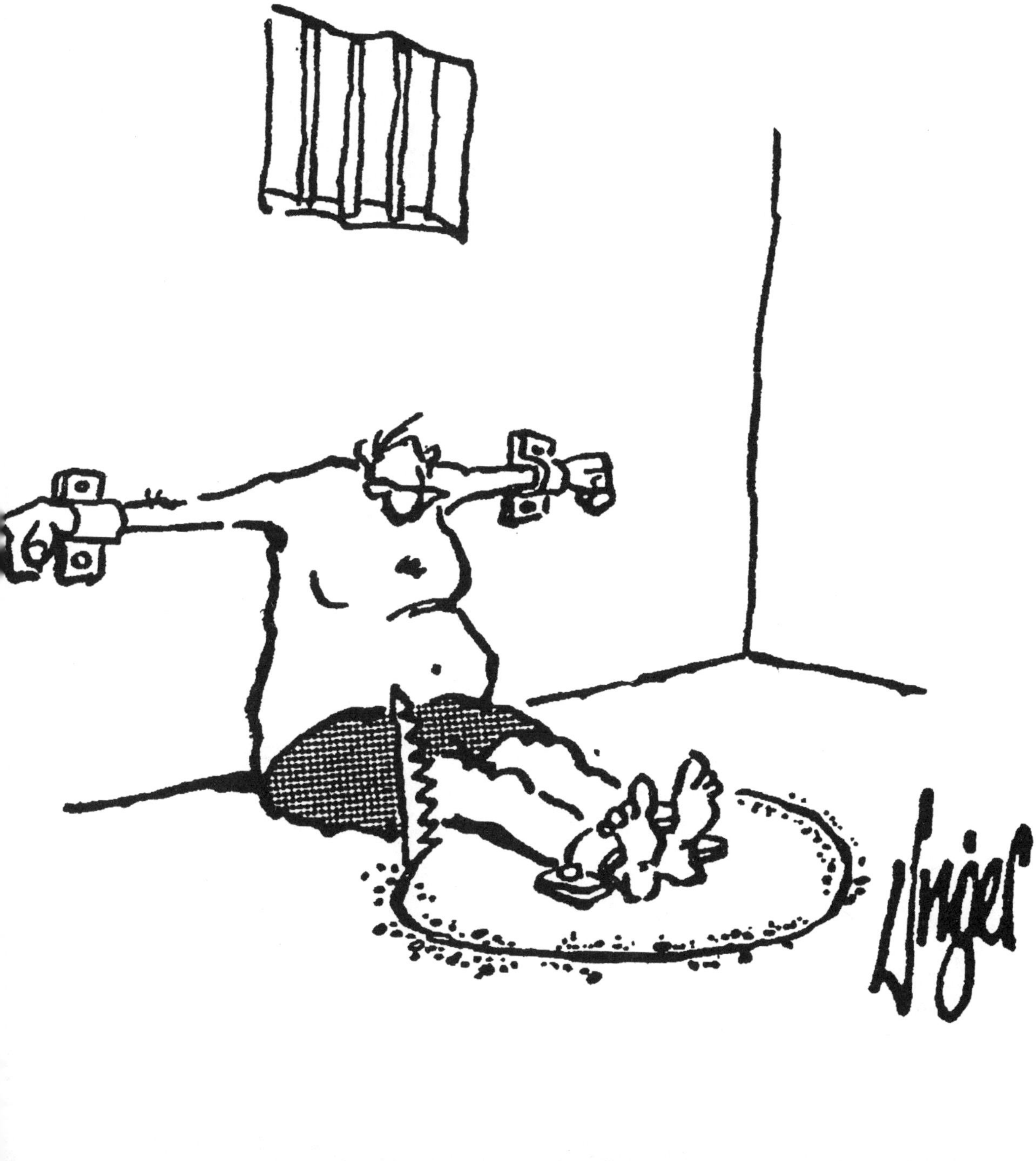
Unger

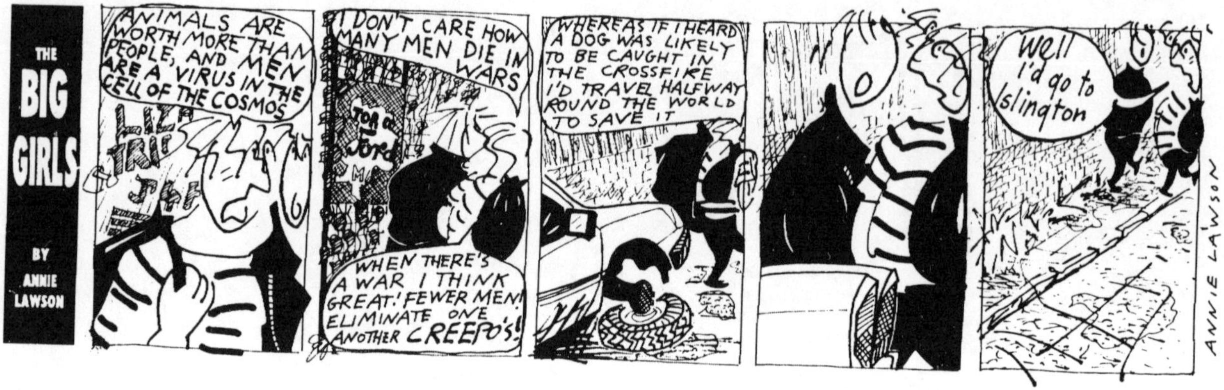
THE BIG GIRLS
BY ANNIE LAWSON
ANIMALS ARE WORTH MORE THAN PEOPLE, AND MEN ARE A VIRUS IN THE CELL OF THE COSMOS
I DON'T CARE HOW MANY MEN DIE IN WARS
WHEN THERE'S A WAR I THINK GREAT! FEWER MEN! ELIMINATE ONE ANOTHER CREEPO'S!
WHEREAS IF I HEARD A DOG WAS LIKELY TO BE CAUGHT IN THE CROSSFIRE I'D TRAVEL HALFWAY ROUND THE WORLD TO SAVE IT
Well i'd go to Islington
ANNIE LAWSON

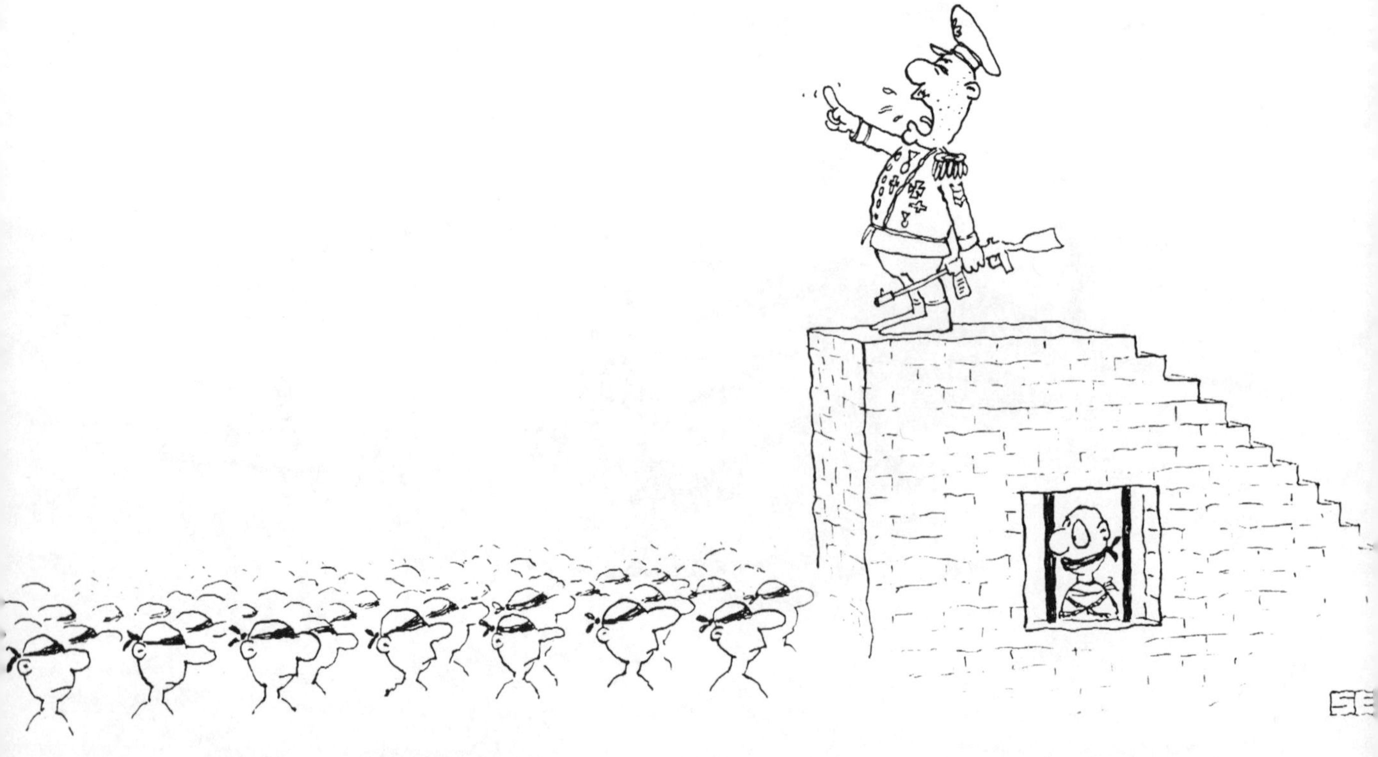

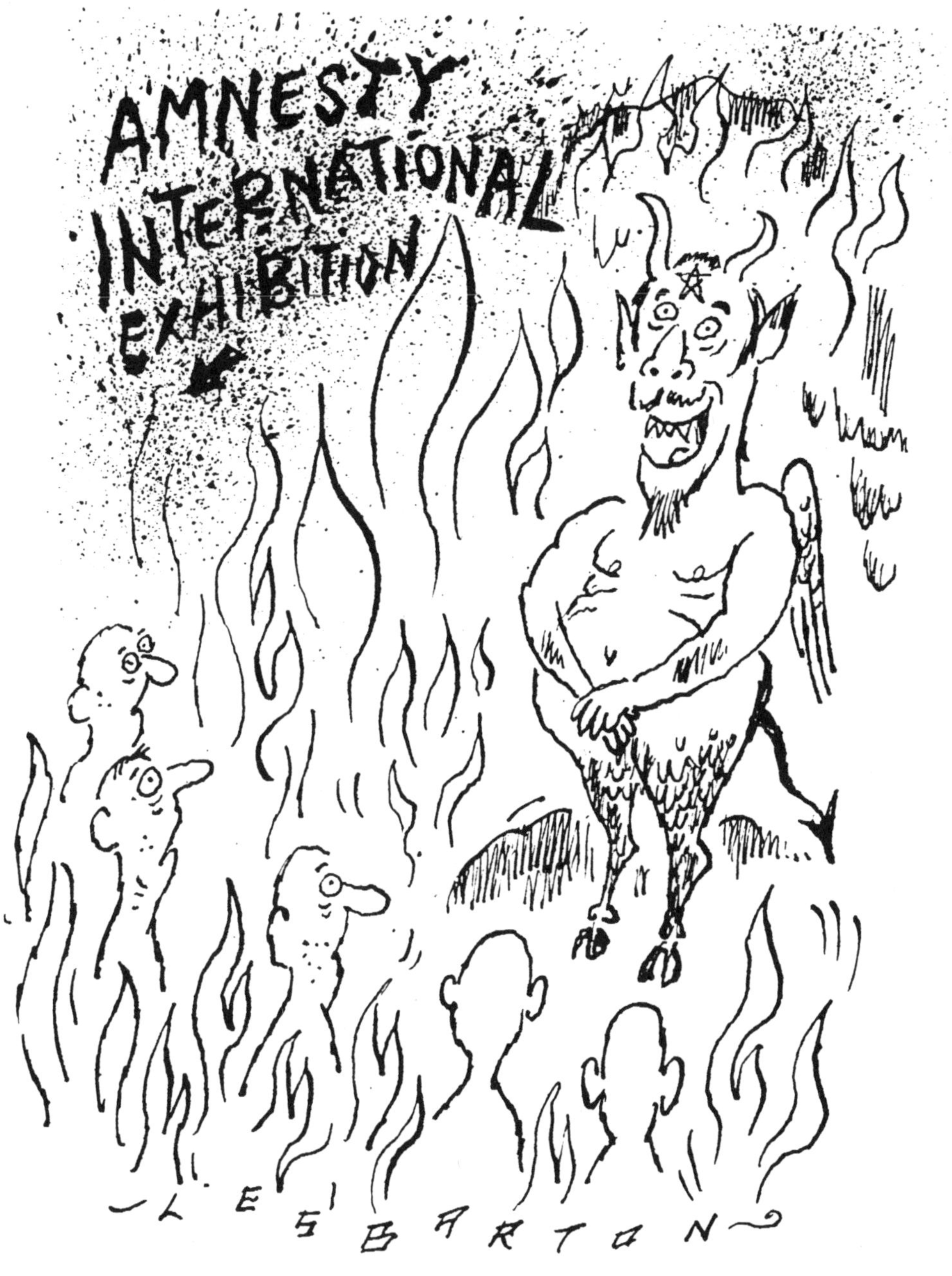
AMNESTY INTERNATIONAL EXHIBITION
LES BARTON

'So in conclusion, I'd like you to join me, in declaring open, this fête worse than death!'

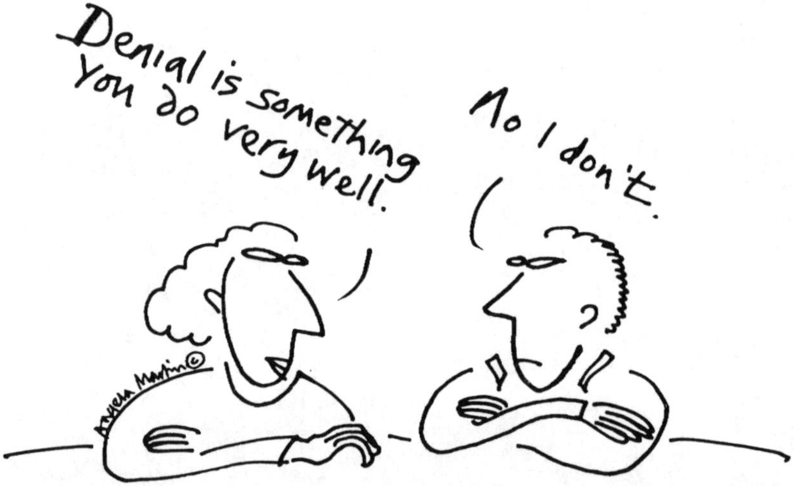
Denial is something you do very well.
No I don't.
Angela Martin©

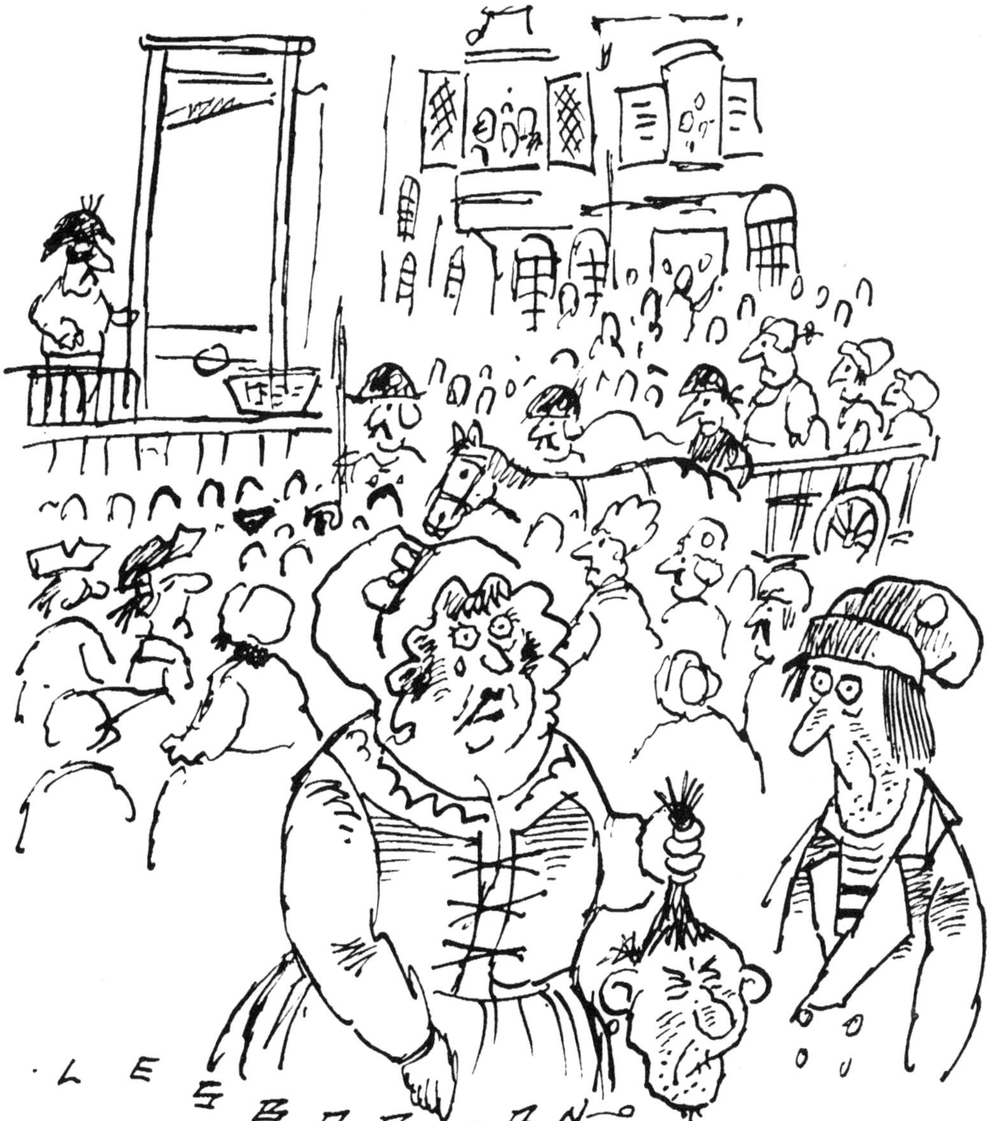
LES BARTON

'After the government has taken their bit this is all I have left!'

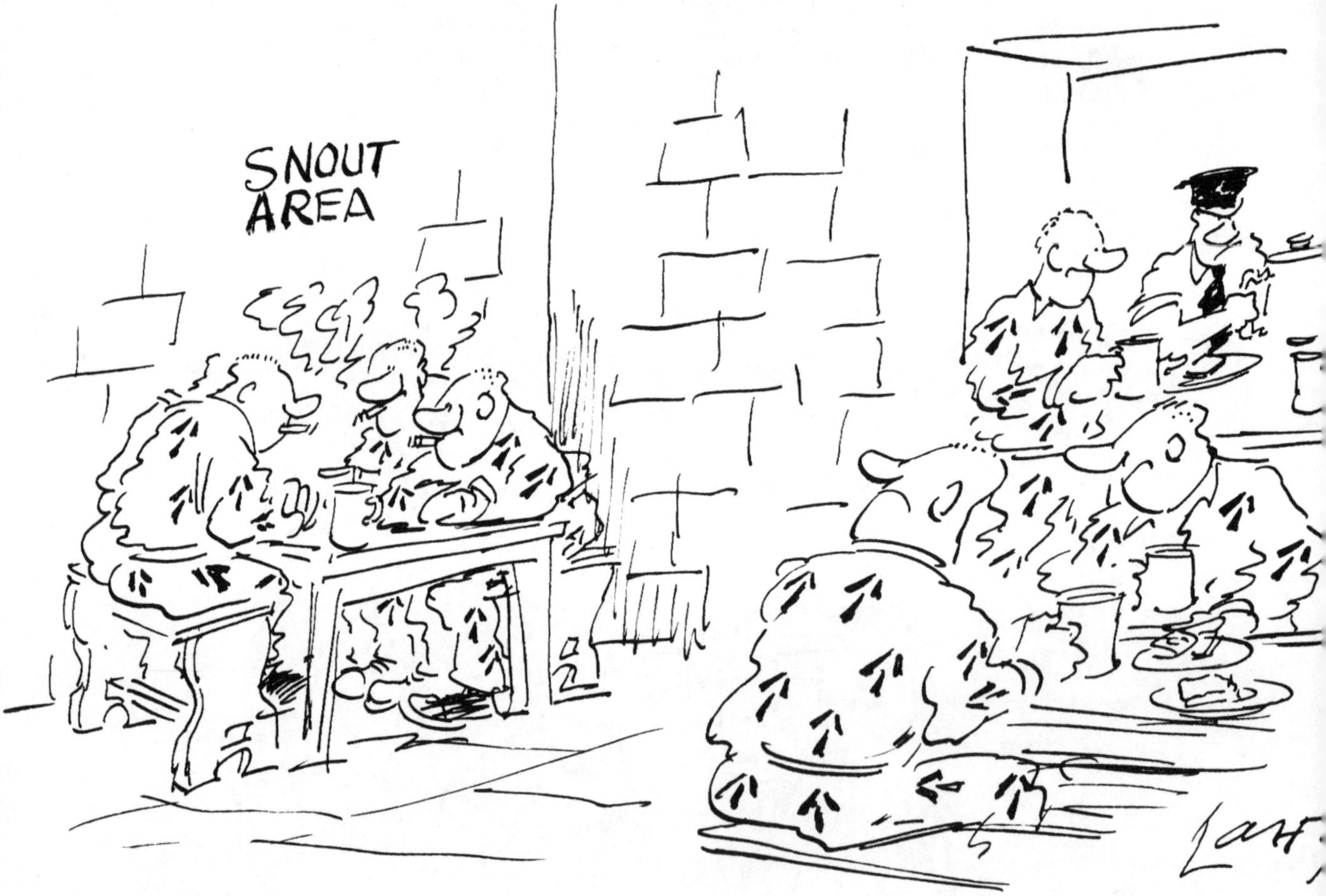
SNOUT
AREA

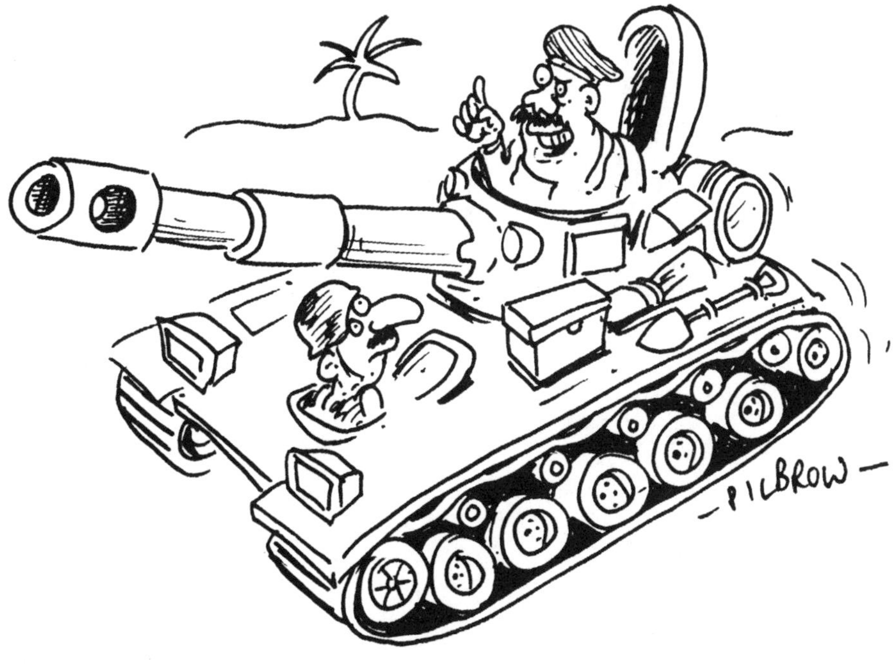
PILBROW

'Don't shoot 'til you see the whites of their flags'

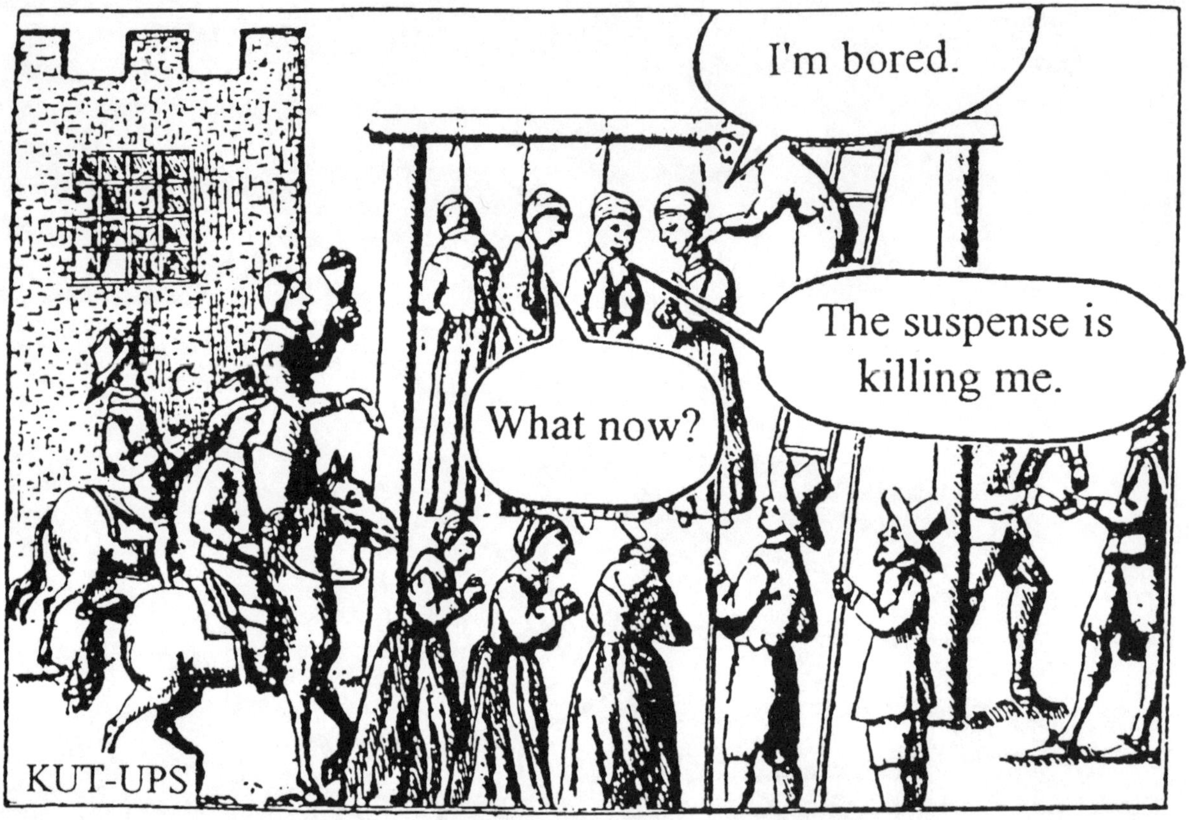
I'm bored.
The suspense is killing me.
What now?
KUT-UPS

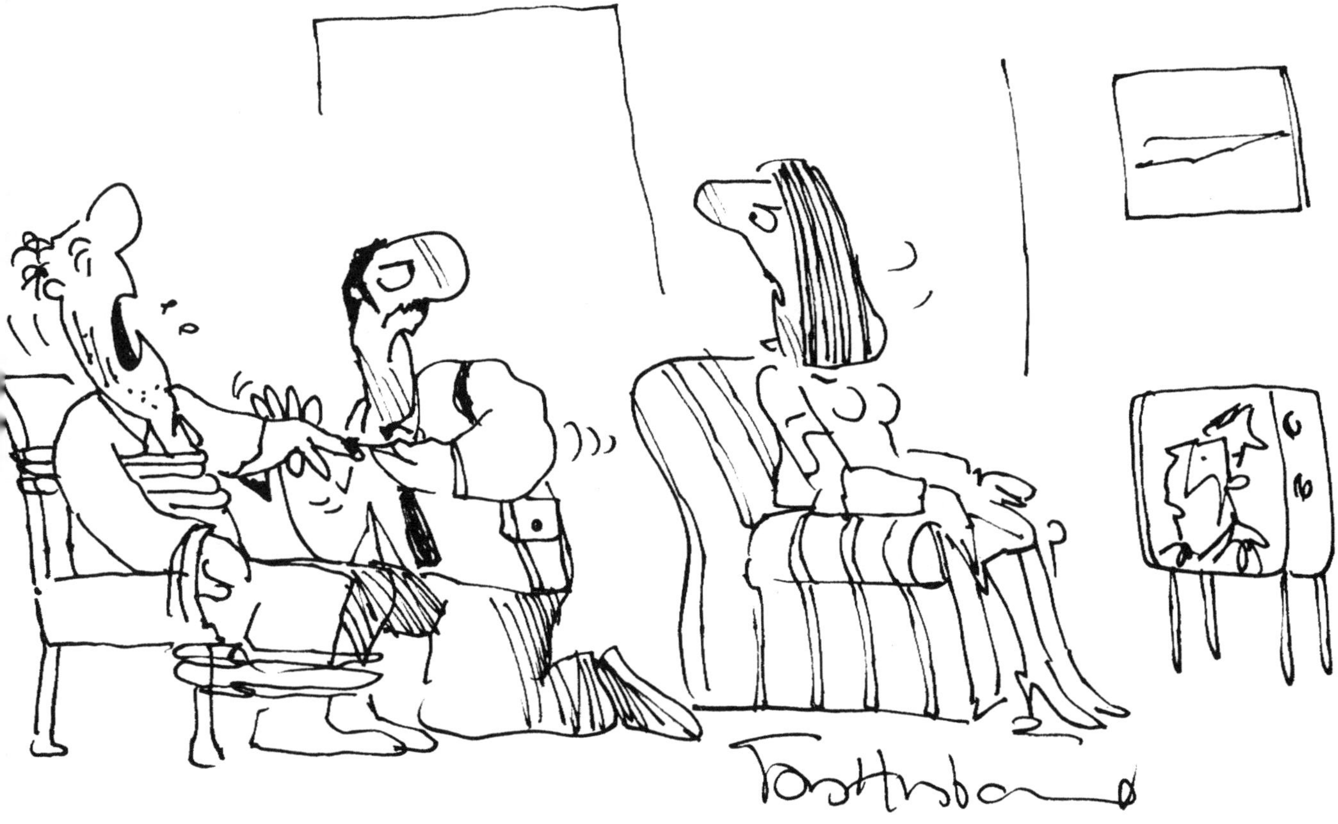

'For God's sake Rodriguez, do you have to bring your work home with you?!'

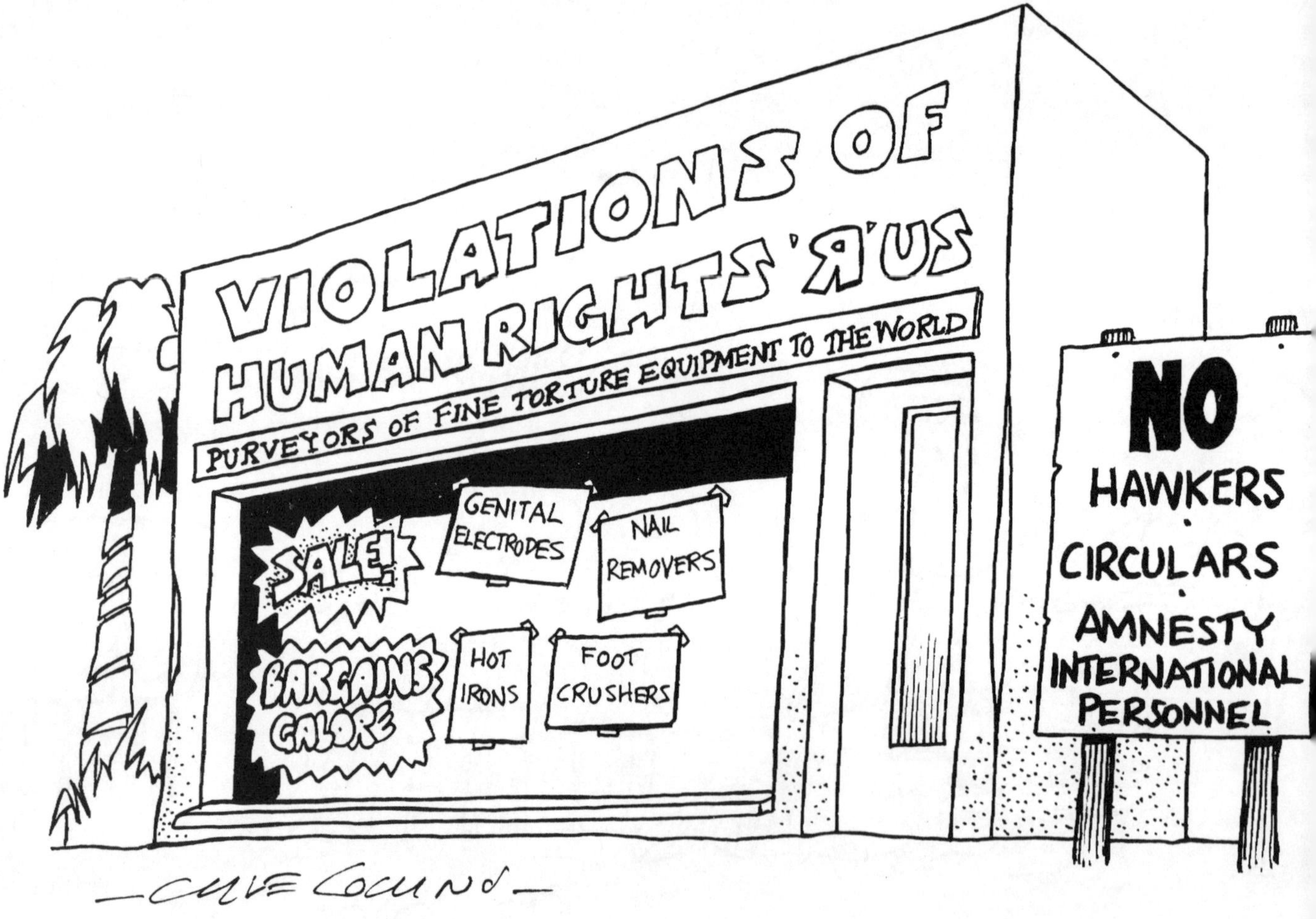
VIOLATIONS OF HUMAN RIGHTS 'Я' US
PURVEYORS OF FINE TORTURE EQUIPMENT TO THE WORLD
SALE!
GENITAL ELECTRODES
NAIL REMOVERS
BARGAINS GALORE
HOT IRONS
FOOT CRUSHERS
NO
HAWKERS
CIRCULARS
AMNESTY INTERNATIONAL PERSONNEL

'Today's topic is **public** awareness'

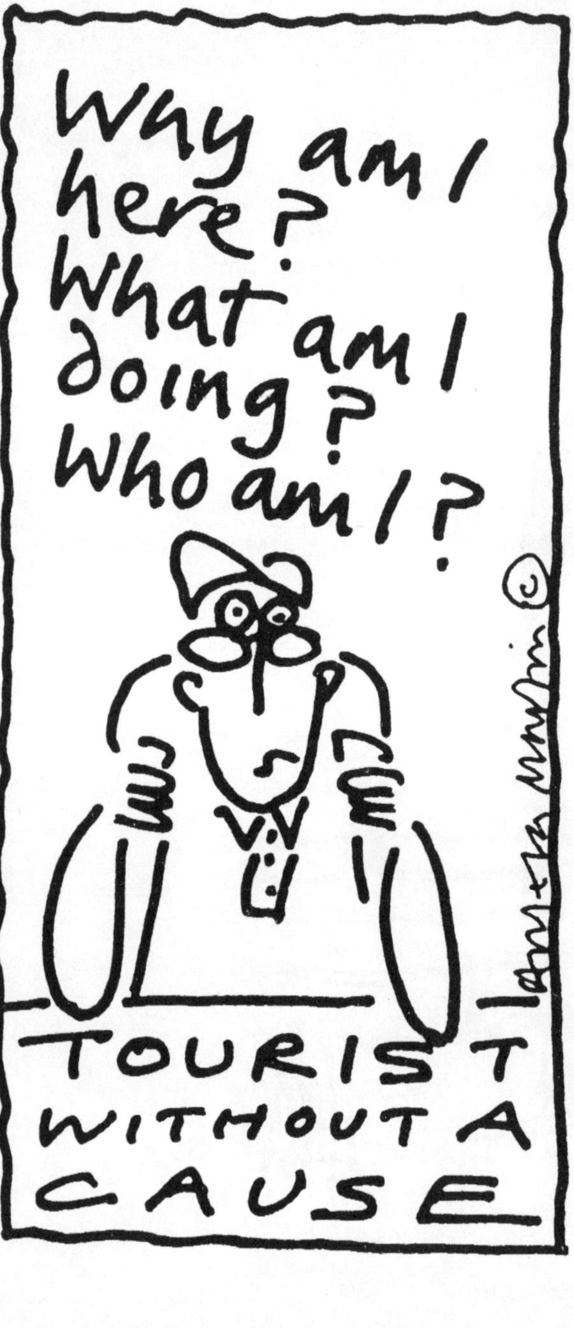
Why am I here? What am I doing? Who am I?
Angela Martin ©
TOURIST WITHOUT A CAUSE

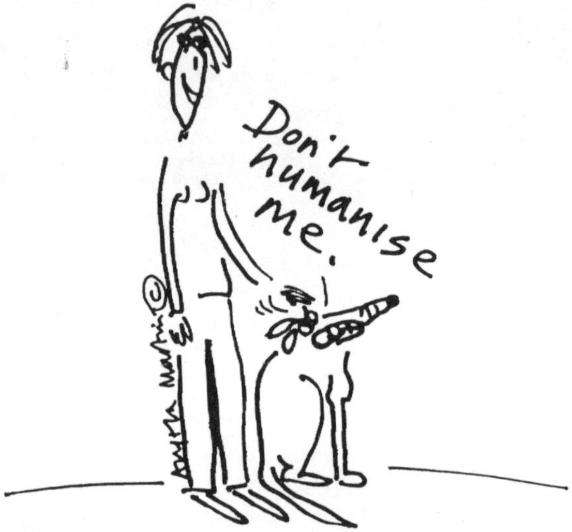
Don't humanise me.

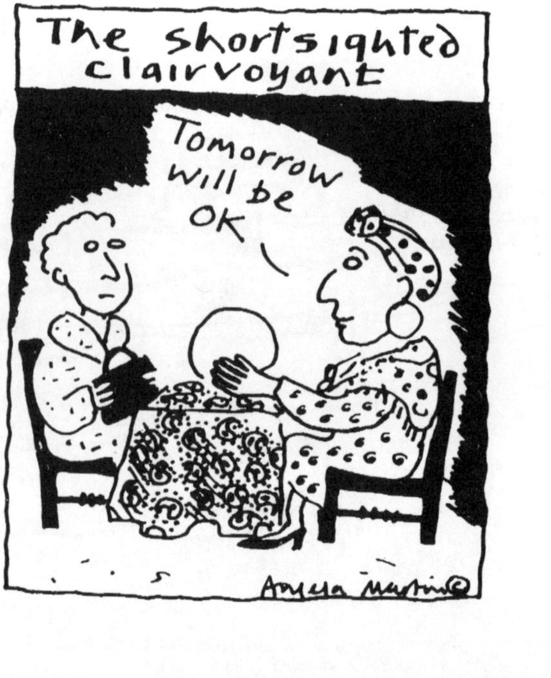
Tomorrow will be OK
Angela Martin ©
The shortsighted clairvoyant

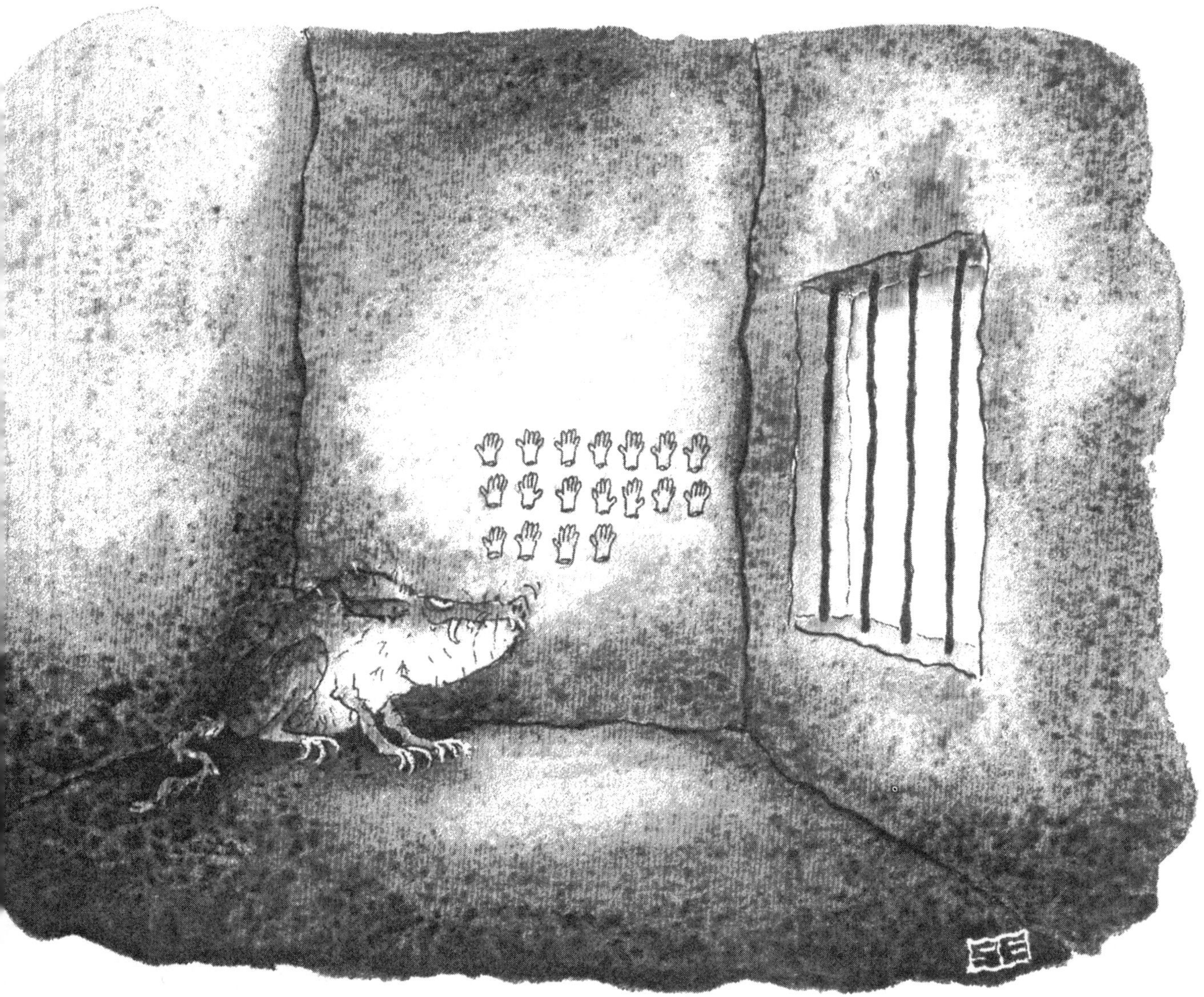

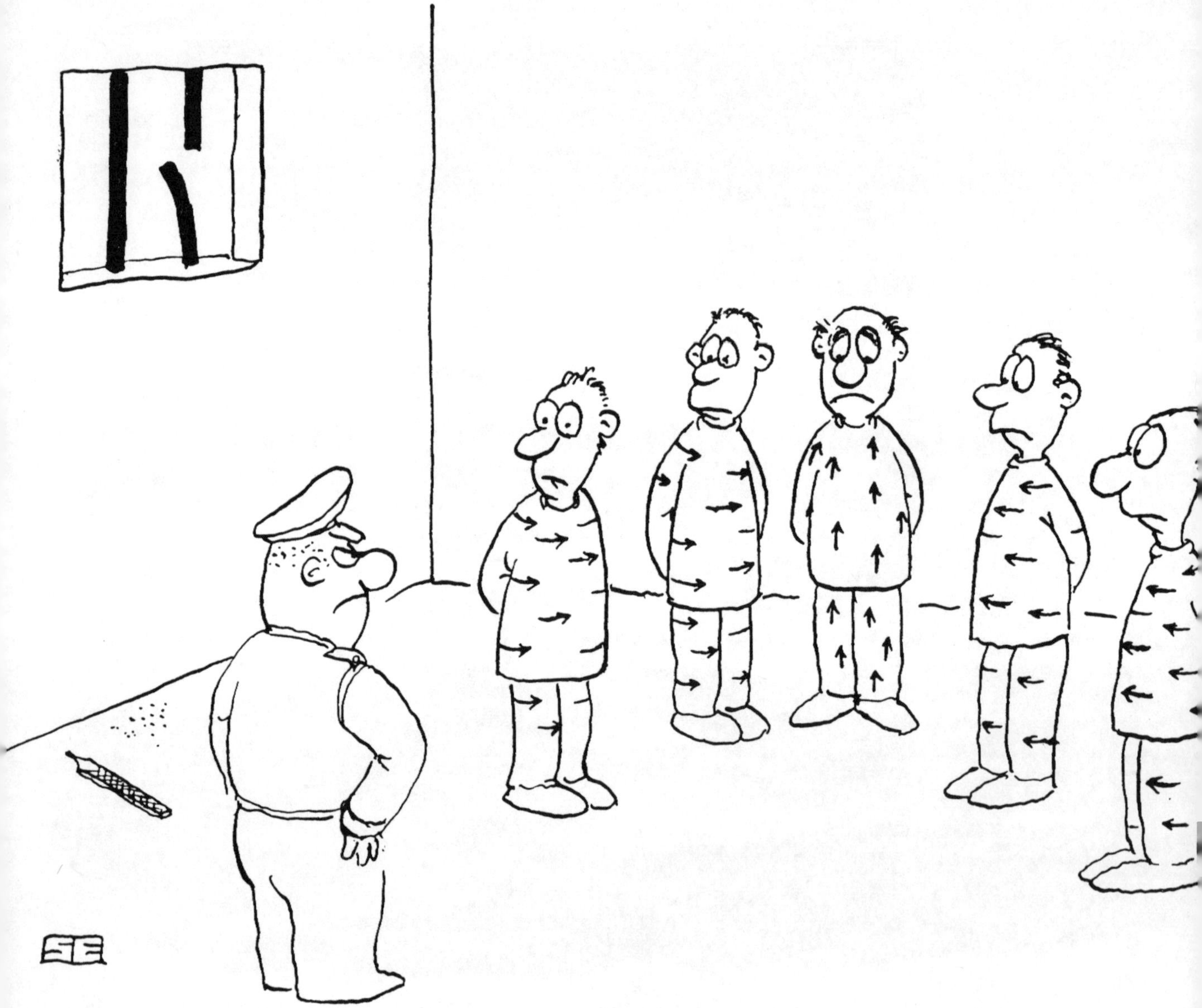
SE

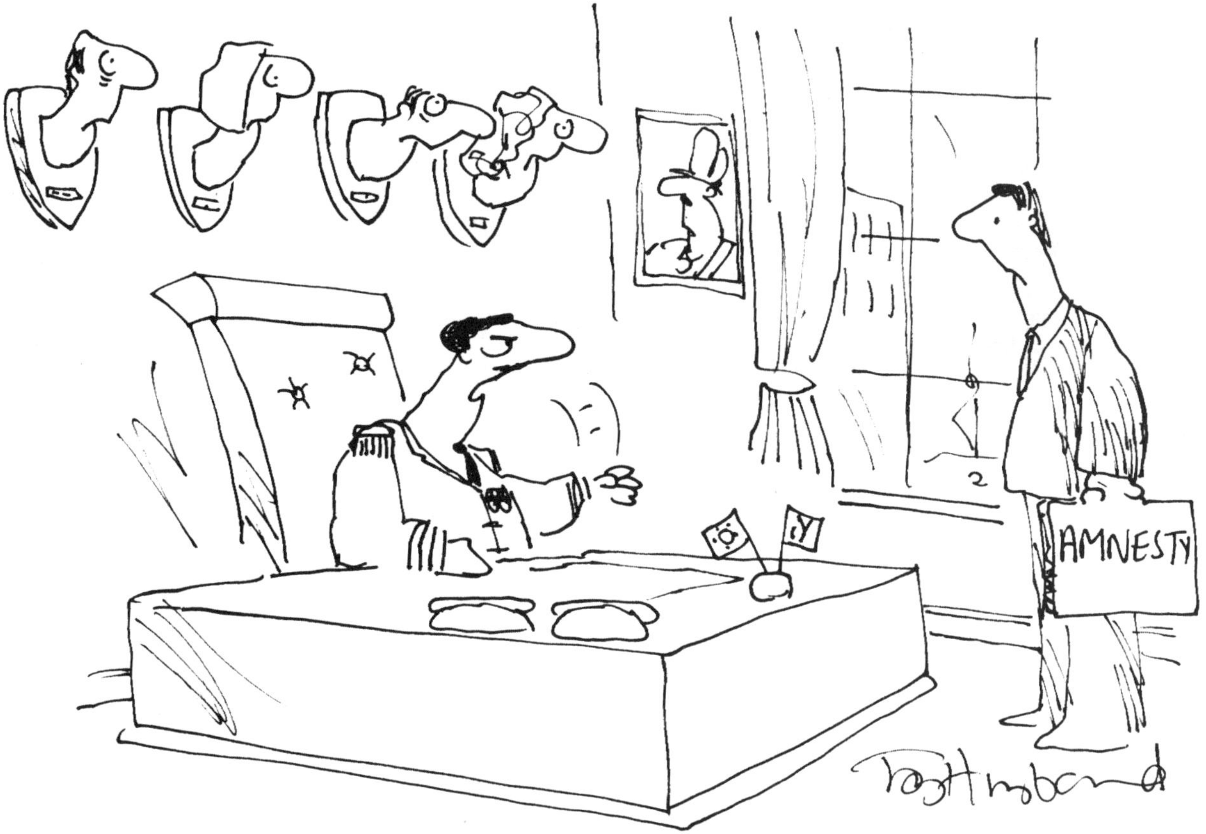
AMNESTY

'How dare you question my country's human rights record!!'

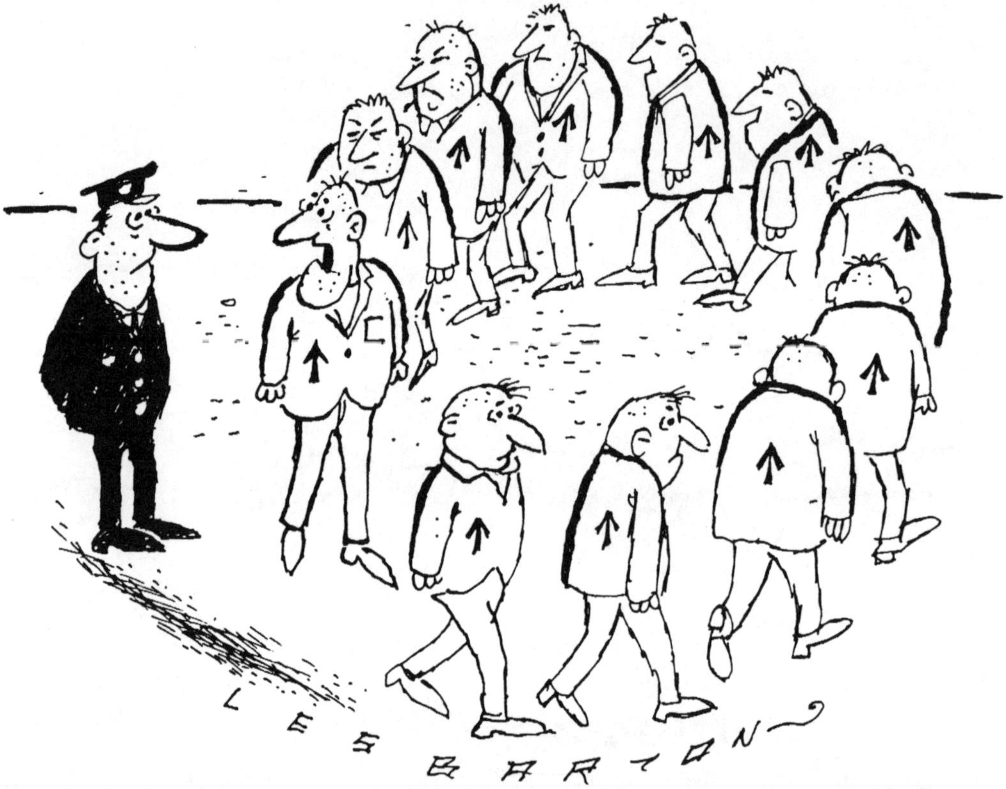
LES BARTON

'I feel tense, sir, can I go the other way to unwind?'

I am not a Human Being, I am a Number.

KUT-UPS

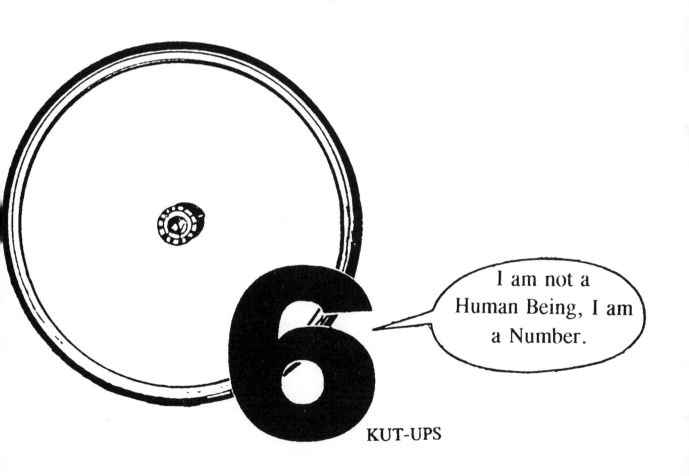

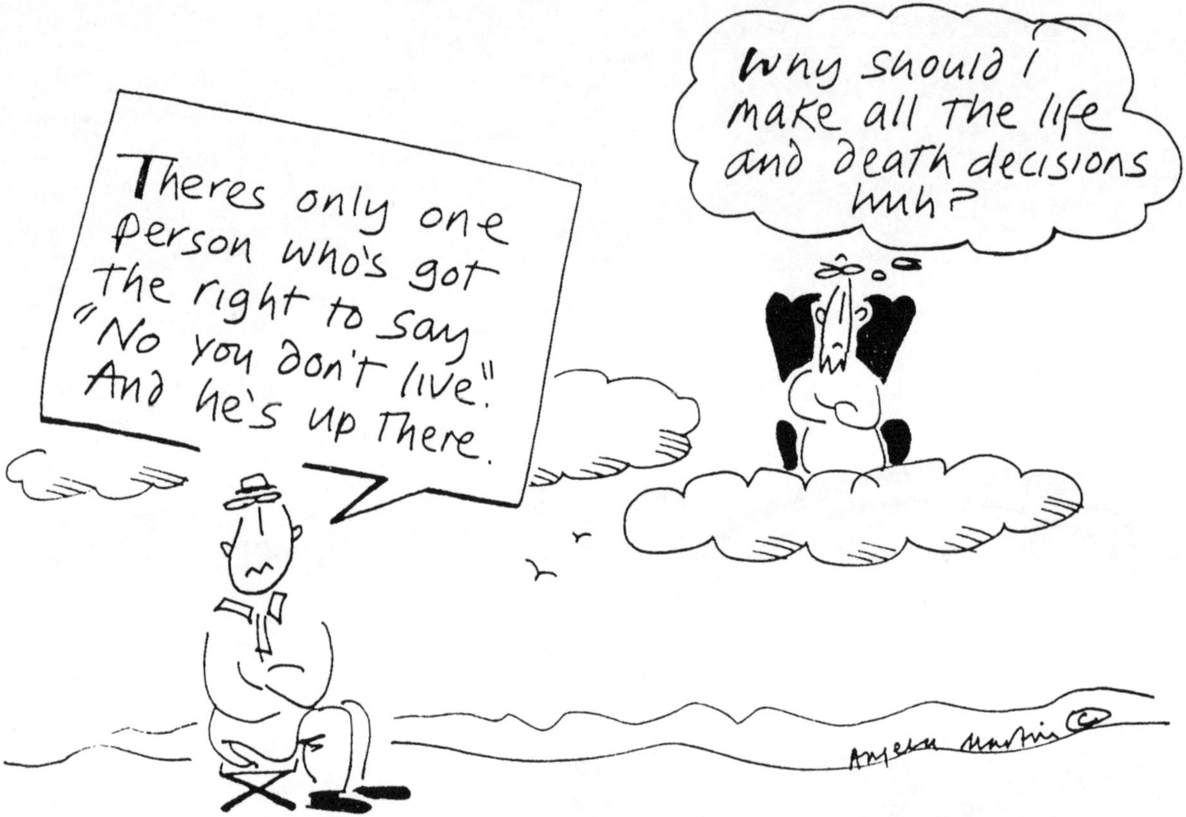

Theres only one person who's got the right to say "No you don't live." And he's up there.
Why should I make all the life and death decisions huh?
Angela Martin ©

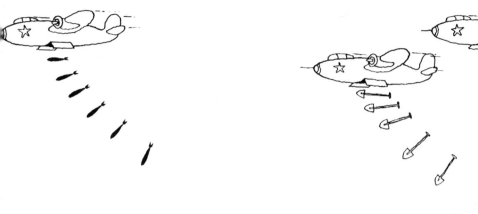
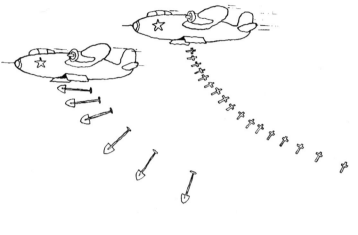

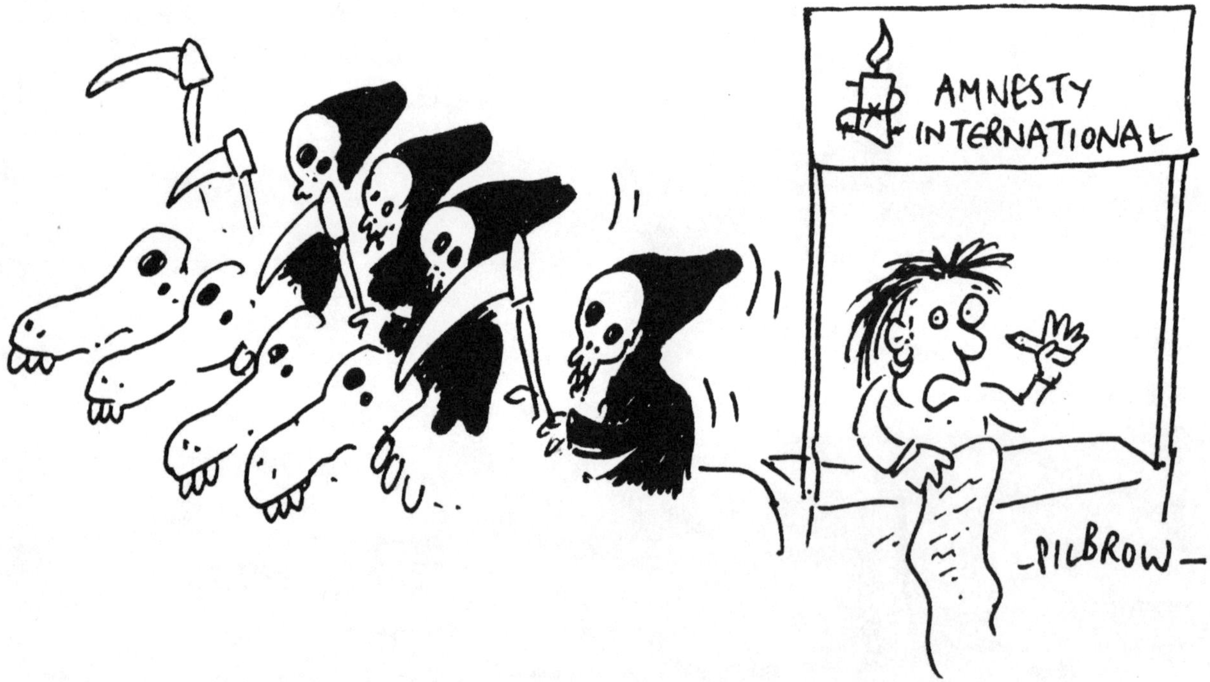
AMNESTY
INTERNATIONAL
-PILBROW-

'Would you gentlemen like to sign our petition? .... I guess not'

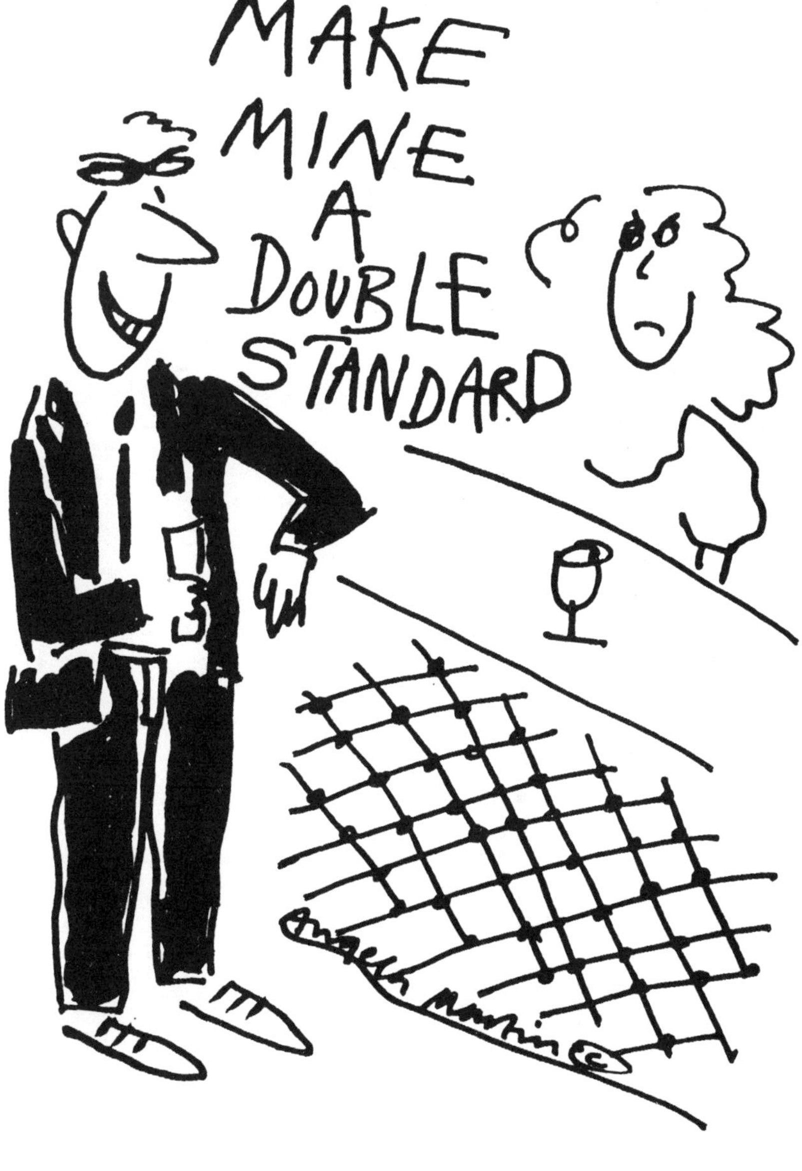
MAKE MINE A DOUBLE STANDARD

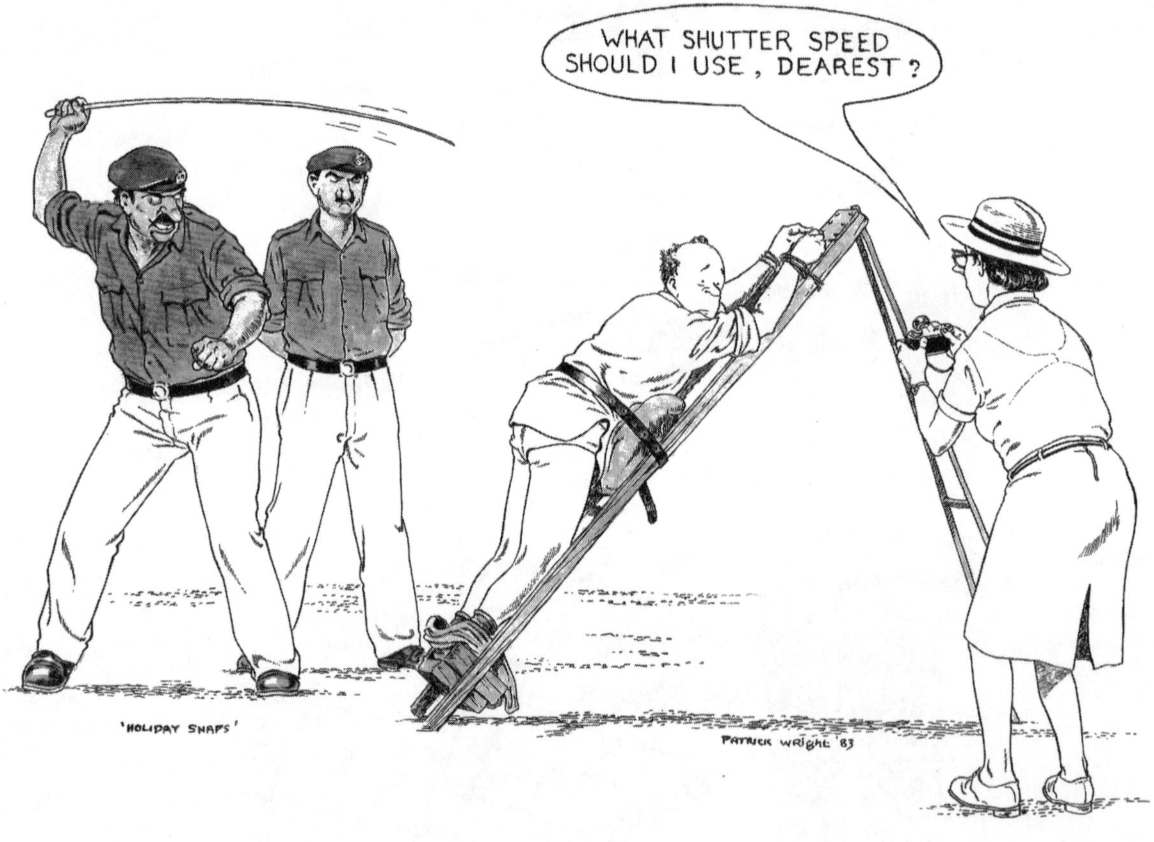
WHAT SHUTTER SPEED
SHOULD I USE, DEAREST?
PATRICK WRIGHT '83
'HOLIDAY SNAPS'

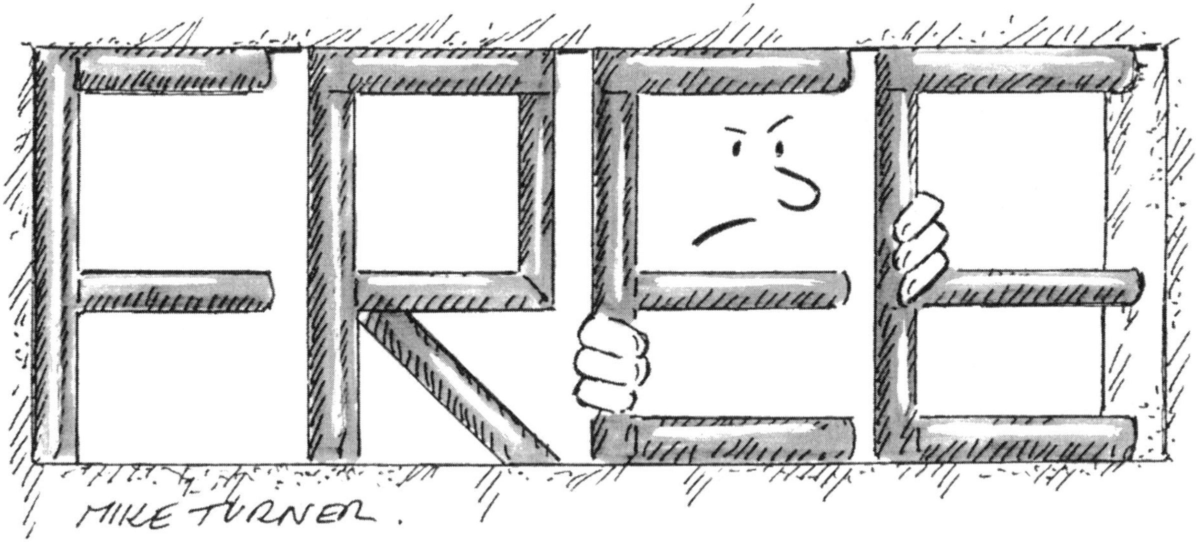
FREE
MIKE TURNER.

MEMBERSHIP

AMNESTY INTERNATIONAL works worldwide for the release of prisoners of conscience, fair trials for political prisoners and an end to torture, extrajudicial executions, "disappearances" and the death penalty.

To join please fill out the form below :

☐ **Family**   £ 27.00   ☐ **Claimant**   £ 7.50

☐ **Individual**   £ 21.00   ☐ **Youth (under 22)**   £ 7.50

☐ **Student**   £ 7.50   ☐ **Senior Citizen**   £ 7.50

I also wish to make a donation of £ _____

Mr/Mrs/Ms . . . . Surname . . . .

Address . . . .

. . . .

Town . . . . County . . . .

Postcode . . . .

Payment method :   You can pay your membership in the following ways :

☐ Cheque   ☐ Postal Order :   Please make payable to Amnesty International

☐ Credit Cards :   Please enter your Access, Visa or Mastercard number below and sign
(if paying by credit card you should give the address where you get your bill)

Valid from . . . .   Valid to . . . .

Signature . . . .   Date . . . .

Please return to :   Membership Department, Amnesty International
99 Rosebery Avenue, London, EC1R 4RE.

94COMCARB/A46